Smarter Study Guides

Instant answers to your most pressing university skills problems.

Are there any secrets to successful study?

The simple answer is no – but there are some essential skills, tips and techniques that can help you to improve your performance and success in all areas of your university studies.

These handy, easy-to-use guides to the most common areas where most students need help (even if you don't realise it!) provide accessible, straightforward practical tips and instant solutions that provide you with the tools and techniques that will enable you to improve your performance and get better results – and better grades!

Each book in the series allows you to assess and address a particular set of skills and strategies, in crucial areas such as exam preparation and performance, researching and writing dissertations and research projects and planning and crafting academic essays. Each book then delivers practical no-nonsense tips, techniques and strategies that will enable you to significantly improve your abilities and performance in time to make a difference.

The books in the series are

- *How to succeed in Exams and Assessments*
- *How to write Essays and Assignments*
- *How to write Dissertations and Project Reports*

Or for a complete handbook covering all of the study skills that you will need throughout your years at university:

- *The Smarter Student: Study Skills and Strategies for Success at University*

Get smart, get a head start!

The Smarter Student series is available at all good bookshops or online at **www.pearson-books.co.uk/studyskills**

Contents

Preface and acknowledgements   vii
How to use this book   ix

Introduction

1 **Why expressing yourself well in writing is important**
 – how to develop your writing skills   3

What markers are looking for

2 **What markers are looking for in your essays and assignments** – how to identify the key elements required to meet markers' expectations   15

Getting started

3 **Tackling writing assignments** – how to get started   29

Researching your topic

4 **Effective academic reading** – how to read efficiently and with understanding   41

5 **The library as a resource** – how to make the best use of the facilities   55

6 **Note-making from texts** – how to create effective notes for later reference   63

7 **Thinking critically** – how to develop a logical approach to analysis, synthesis and evaluation   75

Writing the first draft

8 **Academic writing formats** – how to organise your writing within a standard framework   89

9 **Planning writing assignments** – how to organise your response to the task   95

Writing technique

10 **Academic writing style** – how to adopt the appropriate language conventions ... 105

11 **Shaping your text** – how to create effective sentences and paragraphs ... 115

12 **Improving your grammar** – how to avoid some common errors ... 124

13 **Better punctuation** – how to use punctuation marks appropriately ... 135

14 **Better spelling** – how to spell competently ... 144

15 **Enhancing your vocabulary** – how to increase your word-power ... 152

Editing and revision

16 **Reviewing, editing and proof-reading** – how to make sure your writing is concise and correct ... 167

Plagiarism and referencing

17 **Plagiarism and copyright infringement** – how to avoid being accused of 'stealing' the ideas and work of others ... 179

18 **Citing and listing references** – how to refer appropriately to the work of others ... 189

Presentation

19 **Presentation of assignments** – how to follow the relevant academic conventions ... 209

Improving your marks

20 **Exploiting feedback** – how to improve your marks by learning from what lecturers write on your work ... 223

21 **Essay writing in exams** – how to maximise your marks ... 229

References and further reading ... 239
Glossary ... 240

Preface and acknowledgements

Welcome to *How to Write Essays and Assignments*. We're pleased that you've chosen this book and we hope it will help you with all your academic writing tasks. Our aim has been to provide practical tips to guide you from planning to submission, with help along the way on topics like punctuation, spelling and grammar, so that your work is well developed and meets assessment criteria. We hope the tips we have collated will help you tackle essays and assignments with confidence and produce better results. We've tried to remain faithful to the philosophy of our earlier book, *The Smarter Student*, by creating a quickly accessible resource that you can dip into in time of need. We hope that it will meet your personal needs – regardless of your experience and background.

We would like to offer sincere thanks to many people who have influenced us and contributed to the development and production of this book. Countless students over the years have helped us to test our ideas, especially those whose written work we have commented upon, supervised and assessed. We are grateful to the following colleagues and collaborators who have helped us directly or indirectly: Margaret Adamson, Michael Allardice, John Berridge, Richard Campbell, Margaret Forrest, the late Neil Glen, Anne-Marie Greenhill, Jane Illés, Fiona O'Donnell, Richard Parsons, Mhairi Robb, Anne Scott, Dorothy Smith, Amanda Whitehead and David Wishart. Also, we acknowledge those at other universities who have helped frame our thoughts, particularly our good friends Rob Reed, Nicki Hedge and Esther Daborn. We owe a special debt to the senior colleagues who encouraged various projects that contributed to this book, and who allowed us the freedom to pursue this avenue of scholarship, especially Robin Adamson, Chris Carter, Ian Francis, Rod Herbert and David Swinfen. At Pearson Education, we have had excellent advice and support from Steve Temblett, Georgina Clark-Mazo and Joan Dale Lace. Finally, we would like to say thanks to our long-suffering but nevertheless enthusiastic families: Derek, Keith and Fiona; and Mary, Paul and James, all of whom helped in various capacities.

We'd be delighted to hear your opinion of the book and receive any suggestions you have for additions and improvements.

Kathleen McMillan and Jonathan Weyers
University of Dundee
April 2007

How to use this book

How to Write Essays and Assignments has been organised and designed to be as user-friendly as possible. Each chapter is self-contained and deals with a particular aspect of researching, drafting and writing. You can therefore read the book through from end-to-end, or in sections, or dip into specific chapters as and when you think you need them.

At the start of each chapter you'll find a brief paragraph and a **Key topics** list, which lets you know what's included. There is also a list of *Key terms* at this point, and, should you be uncertain about the meaning of any of these, you will find definitions in the Glossary (pp. 242-7).

Within each chapter, the text is laid out to help you absorb the key concepts easily, using headings and bulleted lists to help you find what you need as efficiently as possible. Relevant examples are contained in figures, tables and boxes, which can be consulted independently, if necessary. The inset boxes are of three types:

 Smart tip boxes emphasise key advice to ensure you adopt a successful approach.

 Information boxes provide additional information, such as useful definitions or examples.

 Query boxes raise questions for you to consider about your personal approach to the topic.

 At the end of each chapter, there's a **Practical tips** section with additional tips. You should regard this as a menu from which to select the ideas that appeal to you and your learning personality.

 Finally, the **And now** box provides three suggestions that you could consider as ideas to take further.

→ Introduction

Why expressing yourself well in writing is important

How to develop your writing skills

Writing an essay or assignment is a challenging and fulfilling activity. It brings together all your relevant knowledge and understanding of a topic in response to a particular task – but it is more than that. From writing tasks, you will gain both an adroitness in use of language and effective communication skills. In addition, you will carry the associated critical thinking skills with you into your professional life after university. This chapter outlines the importance of developing your ability to express yourself well in written assignments; a contribution to your training as a wordsmith.

Key topics:

→ Making sure that you have the necessary writing skills
→ Intellect and writing
→ Writing as part of the process of communication
→ Taking a long-term view

Key terms
Critical thinking   Genres   Register

Writing is something that will not be confined to your university days. Indeed, your ability to use the transferable skill of writing will mark you out as a competent communicator of facts and opinions. In your professional life, in all sorts of contexts and for all sorts of purposes, you will draw on the training you receive at university in presenting your ideas effectively on paper. Thus, writing well is an integral facet of the skills set that you take away with you from the university experience. However, it takes time and dedication to acquire and develop the facility in writing that you'll need. This means that the act of writing essays will help you to hone your writing skill into an effective tool of communication.

Writing to express ideas can only be achieved if you have the right skills at your disposal. You need to heed the practicalities of locating relevant material, researching information, and checking so that you will be able to extract what is relevant to your purpose. Once you have this information, you need to organise and structure it to meet the requirements of your task. From this starting point, you then need to learn to 'play' with language. Apart from avoiding the obvious errors of grammar, punctuation and spelling, you need to experiment with each choice of word, each grouping, the ordering of words, and the construction of each sentence and paragraph (Table 1.1). This focus on manipulating writing is important for a number of reasons:

- it demonstrates your ability to group ideas in a logical way;
- it allows you to exploit the flexibility that language offers you to express your thoughts as clearly as possible; and
- it ensures that you maintain the reader's attention and interest.

Table 1.1 provides several examples of ways in which language can be manipulated to improve communication.

Developing your writing skills

Chapters that relate to improving your competence in writing are:

- Effective academic reading (**Ch 4**)
- The library as a resource (**Ch 5**)
- Academic writing formats (**Ch 8**)
- Academic writing style (**Ch 10**)
- Shaping your paragraph (**Ch 11**)
- Improving your grammar (**Ch 12**)
- Better punctuation (**Ch 13**)
- Better spelling (**Ch 14**)
- Enhancing your vocabulary (**Ch 15**)

Table 1.1 Examples of how 'playing with language' can improve your writing. Writing can often be improved by rearranging the order of words or phrases, by choosing more suitable words or by separating out ideas into independent elements. Examples A-C below illustrate possible techniques that you might adopt.

A. Heads and tails
Sometimes a sentence works better if you experiment by shifting elements around within it. A phrase or clause that is at the tail end of the sentence might be more powerful, and emphasise your meaning more strongly, if it is positioned at the head of the sentence. For example:
Version A1: *The practical application of 'duty to disclose' in relation to the onset of multiple sclerosis was deliberately entrusted to the discretion of the medical profession **because it was seen as impossible to define in policy**.*
could become
Version A2: ***Since it was considered impossible to define 'duty to disclose' in policy** in relation to the onset of multiple sclerosis, the practical application was deliberately entrusted to the medical profession.*
Both instances have validity. However, as a writer, you might wish to place the emphasis on the reason for the failure to define a policy. In that case, Version A2 would be better. However, if you felt the emphasis should rest with the role of the medical profession, then Version A1 would be better. This shows the importance of considering your intention as you construct and review your writing, and it emphasises how important applying logic is to the whole process.
B. Better word, clearer meaning
Academic writing should, by definition, be both precise and concise. However, sometimes in the process of writing the need to record the ideas overtakes the accuracy and clarity that might be desirable. Consequently, it is worthwhile reviewing your work to identify ways in which you can use words more appropriately to achieve clarity. For example:
Version B1: *The practical application of 'duty to disclose' in relation to the onset of multiple sclerosis was deliberately entrusted to **the decision-making process operating** in the medical profession because it was seen as impossible to define in policy.*
could become
Version B2: *The practical application of 'duty to disclose' in relation to the onset of multiple sclerosis was deliberately entrusted to the **discretion** of the medical profession because it was seen as impossible to define in policy.*
Not only is Version B2 clearer than Version B1, but it expresses more aptly the leeway that the situation implies.

▶

Table 1.1 continued

C. Long and short sentences
Sometimes it is better to split an overly long or complex sentence. For example:
Version C1: *The practical application of 'duty to disclose' in relation to the onset of multiple sclerosis was deliberately entrusted to the discretion of the medical profession* **because it was seen as impossible to define in policy.**
could become
Version C2: *The practical application of 'duty to disclose' in relation to the onset of multiple sclerosis was deliberately entrusted to the discretion of the medical profession.* **This decision was reached because it was seen as impossible to define in policy.**
Version C1 places the reason as a tag on the end of the main clause, whereas Version C2 emphasises the reason by stating it as a separate sentence.

Although it is possible to enjoy the luxury of writing well when there is time to polish the finished version of essays and other assignments written over a reasonably long time frame, there may not be the same opportunity to indulge this attention to detail under examination conditions. Nevertheless, the practice gained constructing essays within the scheme of your coursework develops the skill of writing which helps you to write well under pressure within the time limits of exams.

→ Intellect and writing

Writing is an expression of logic that is the product of thinking. Thus, the writing that you produce is a reflection of your intellectual abilities. It puts into words your knowledge and your conceptual understanding and shows evidence of your critical thinking. Furthermore, it demonstrates your competence in expressing higher-order concepts in ways that, for example, show your ability to:

- provide evidence of your problem-solving abilities;
- construct arguments and counter-arguments;
- engage with the higher-order thinking of others and to integrate the essence of that thinking into your own work; and
- express opinions based on sound analysis, synthesis and evaluation of multiple sources.

Often problems of writing stem from lack of logic and this can be overcome by planning the structure of the entire text as well as the paragraphs and sentences that it contains.

It would be an exceptional author who could write fluently and without error at the first attempt. Therefore, offering your material to a 'study buddy', friend or family member for comment can provide insights into areas where your logic has slipped either in expression or rationale. Learning to accept criticism of your writing from others helps you to develop skills in refining your thoughts and your use of language. Ultimately, you should aim to be self-critical as part of the writing process.

Demonstrating your higher-order skills in writing

Chapters that relate to demonstrating your intellectual ability in writing are:

- Tackling writing assignments (**Ch 3**)
- Thinking critically (**Ch 7**)
- Planning writing assignments (**Ch 9**)
- Plagiarism and copyright infringement (**Ch 17**)
- Citing and listing references (**Ch 18**)

→ Writing as part of the process of communication

If writing is the product of thought it is also a vehicle for communicating that thought to others. Communicating your ideas in writing is important because:

- it shows that you can meet the expectations and marking criteria of those who grade your work;
- it demonstrates your intellectual abilities to others;
- it identifies you as a higher-order thinker who can engage with more sophisticated ideas;
- it demonstrates your ability to analyse and explain complex ideas to others; and
- it illustrates your competence as an effective communicator to future employers.

Demonstrating good communication skills in writing

Chapters that relate to demonstrating your ability to absorb information and communicate well in writing are:

- What markers are looking for in your essays and assignments (**Ch 2**)
- Note-making from texts (**Ch 6**)
- Academic writing style (**Ch 10**)
- Reviewing, editing and proof-reading (**Ch 16**)
- Presentation of assignments (**Ch 19**)

Without the combination of effective use of writing skills and your intellectual abilities, you will have limited success in communicating your ideas to others. This may mean that the effort you expend on producing your essays may not be reflected in good grades. Attributes of your academic writing that can impede or enhance the communicative effectiveness of your essays include:

- **Register.** To express yourself well in writing, you need to be aware that the form of communication that you might use in speech is not suitable for the more formal 'register' of academic essay-writing (**Ch 10**). Register relates to the level of informality or formality that can sometimes impede communication. A piece of text that is written in an informal manner may fail to communicate ideas for a number of reasons:
  - Informal language is, by its very nature, limited and imprecise and can resort to use of transient slang expressions which may rapidly become dated and obsolete.
  - Since informal language is closely related to speech, there is a greater likelihood that it will be more emotive and less objective in its tone.
  - Informality in writing may not be seen as a serious attempt at responding to the essay task. (On the other hand, an essay written in an over-complex register with a style of language that is convoluted or archaic is just as likely to impede understanding and effective communication.)

Carefully worded text, using well-constructed sentences and paragraphs appropriate to the understanding and ability of your audience, is more likely to communicate ideas well; and, in terms of essays, is more likely to earn you good grades.

● **Objectivity.** If you want to communicate clearly in written assignments, then it is important to adopt a style of writing that conveys your ideas in a way that presents an objective perspective on the topic (**Ch 10**). If you provide your readers with a subjectively worded commentary, then they will be less likely to consider your work a professional piece of writing. It is possible to write in a detached way, yet convey that the views are personal.

→ Taking a long-term view

Developing your skill in academic writing is a challenging process. It requires time and patience to learn from the drafting, crafting, and redrafting that is part of the evolutionary passage of every assignment from rough notes to final version. As you gain expertise in critiquing your own writing, you will gain confidence in your ability to produce good, well-expressed text. In addition, each criticism you receive, whether from colleagues or from teaching staff, will help you to refine and enhance your skill as an autonomous and effective academic communicator and author.

Practical tips for expressing yourself well in writing

Become more aware of the different registers of writing. Writing a message on a holiday postcard is an informal sort of communication; however, writing an essay or professional report invites a more formal approach. Scrutinise your writing to ensure that you use language and structures that are well suited to the more formal style and vocabulary expected at university.

Learn more about the writing styles used in your subject area. A commonly held view is that there are considerable differences in the writing styles employed in different disciplines. While this will clearly be the case in terms of content, the style of writing will be governed by good use of standard English, written clearly and without ambiguity – and this holds true for all disciplines. Long words, long sentences and long paragraphs do not necessarily add up to messages that are written clearly. Become familiar with the writing of some of the experts in your field and examine their texts to help you decide what makes their writing powerful and expressive.

Learn more about how you are expected to write within your target profession. Many of the tasks you will be asked to undertake at university are designed to prepare you for writing in your professional life. Once you graduate you will probably need to adapt your writing skills further in order to meet the 'house style' of your employer or, perhaps, the style expected by your professional body. Again, seeking out and surveying some such professional material – for example, in-house journals, reports or printed publicity – will help to give you an understanding of what you might be expected to produce.

Develop deliberate strategies to help expand your vocabulary. Acquiring a good command of the specialist terminology, or jargon, used in your specific field is essential to your academic writing, but these words and phrases represent only a small part of the language that you will need to express your ideas with flair and confidence. For this reason, expanding your vocabulary is a good way to enhance your skill as a writer. So often, the different nuances that need to be explained in a text can be lost simply because of the rather limited range of words that writers have at their disposal. Reading widely within your own field and beyond can help to develop this aspect of your personal ability.

Spend some time looking at how you can meet the expectations of markers. Bringing your work up to standard could be as simple as learning some of the more sophisticated grammatical rules, making yourself aware of some of the finer points of punctuation, or learning some fairly routine aspects of presentation. These are the sorts of things that markers expect to be part of the skills set that students should possess and so, if you can identify the areas in which you might improve the way you write and how you present your writing, you may be able to improve your grades.

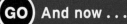

GO And now . . .

1.1 Look at your present work and compare the writing with work you did some time ago. Look for ways in which your writing is evolving as your studies progress. What sorts of things have changed? What might you strive to change to make your writing more expressive and effective?

1.2 Learn more about language. By using your writing skills to make contributions to your university students' newspaper or by joining a creative writing class, you will have an opportunity to learn about how language works and how it can be used to good effect in different genres. This will help you to develop as a writer and also provide you with constructive feedback from other more experienced writers.

1.3 Think about your writing skills in context of employment. Look at job advertisements in professional journals or national newspapers. See how often posts advertised require applicants with 'good communication skills'. This includes the skill of writing so you should consider just how confidently you could state that your writing skills might meet these requirements and how you might provide evidence of this. If you feel your writing skills could be improved, then much of the material in this book could be of value as you develop your ability and create a portfolio of evidence to support your applications.

→ **What markers are looking for**

2 What markers are looking for in your essays and assignments

How to identify the key elements required to meet markers' expectations

When your lecturers and tutors assign a grade to your work they are looking for a relevant response to the task that has been set in the essay or assignment. They will be looking for features that distinguish your work as competent and appropriate to your level of study within the context of the course or module you are taking. This chapter outlines the sorts of things that will contribute to your final grade, but also covers aspects that could lose you credit with the marker.

Key topics:
→ Course guidance material
→ How written assignments are marked
→ What markers are looking for in terms of presentation
→ What markers are looking for in terms of structure
→ What markers are looking for in terms of content
→ How essay feedback can help you to improve your future grades

Key terms
Anonymous marking   External examiner   Feedback
Formative assessment   Learning outcome   Learning objective
Marking criteria   Marking scheme   Primary source
Secondary source   Syllabus

Markers are generally influenced by three dimensions of a student's essay writing: the presentation, the structure and the content. The marker will assess the quality of your answer by reference to explicit and implicit marking criteria that relate to these dimensions. You can find out about the broader criteria against which your work will be judged by looking more closely at your course guide or handbook.

→ Course guidance material

Course guides and handbooks may be provided in hard copy, or posted on your course module within your institution's virtual learning environment. They usually include:

- **Generic information.** This includes assessment or reporting scales for assignments (often with grading criteria); particular citation and referencing formats; information about word limits (and whether any appendices are included in the word count); presentation and submission information; and penalties for late submission. There may also be some basic advice on writing style and conventions that may apply in your discipline.

- **Syllabus information and learning objectives or outcomes.** To understand more particularly what the marker is looking for, you need to look at two more detailed parts of the course guide – the course syllabus and the related learning objectives (sometimes called 'outcomes'). In an ideal world, the learning objectives should relate to the way the topic is assessed. Depending on how the syllabus is structured and delivered, you may find that the objectives are outlined for the whole course, that each theme within the syllabus has its own learning objectives, or both. Although some learning objectives are worded so that they do not provide detailed guidance, properly constructed objectives will give you a well-defined 'steer' on what the markers will be looking for in assignments, particularly if you map these on to the elements from the courses that are relevant to the task you have been set.

→ How written assignments are marked

Many students pay little attention to the events that lead to a grade being given to their work. However, it is important to understand this process if you wish to meet the expectations of the markers and be awarded a good mark. Here are some of the questions and answers you should be taking into account:

- **Who marks your work?** The person who marks your work is not always the academic who delivered the lecture content of the course. The marker will, however, have an expertise in the discipline and be well acquainted with the theme of the assignment. To ensure that fairness is applied to the grading system, papers may be 'double-marked' anonymously. This means that they are marked by a second marker, generally from within the department. If the assignment is critical to a degree classification, or if there has been a difference between the grades allocated by the first and second markers, the paper may be sent for adjudication by the external marker.

- **How do markers decide on your grade?** A number of factors will contribute to deciding your grade, but these may differ from subject to subject and assignment to assignment. To a certain extent, all markers reach their decision about a grade intuitively, on the basis of their professional experience and expertise as academics; however, to ensure that their decision is objective and that students are treated fairly and equally, they will often refer to marking scales reflecting a list of generalised (departmental) marking criteria, such as those shown below and in Tables 2.1 and 2.2. In some cases, and especially where double-marking occurs, these may be further refined into a marking scheme for a specific question, which details what proportion of marks will be given to each particular aspect of your submission.

Marking criteria

These are defined in course handbooks and explain what has to be achieved in order to attain particular grades. They differ from module to module, discipline to discipline and level to level. Thus, it is important to read them with care in order to identify the standards you hope to reach. In the top band for a module assignment, such criteria might state that assessed work should:

- Contain all the information required with no or very few errors.
- Show evidence of having read relevant literature and use this effectively in the answer.
- Address the question correctly, understanding all its nuances.
- Contain little or no irrelevant material.
- Demonstrate full understanding of the topic within a wider context.
- Show good critical and analytical abilities.
- Contain evidence of sound independent thinking.
- Express ideas clearly and concisely.
- Use appropriate written structure and good standard of English.
- Present diagrams, where required, that are detailed and relevant.

Table 2.1 Numerical (percentage) marking scale with sample marking criteria for different grade classifications. Institutions vary about how coursework is graded. However, the marking criteria shown below will have some kind of correspondence with the system that applies in your institution and you should be able to find this information in your course handbook or guide.

Honours classification	Grade	Numerical mark	Marking criteria
First Class Honours	Grade A	70–100% (note that in some universities, this grade is split into two bands)	Work at this level will show an outstanding command of the material, a high level of the awareness of issues, developments and critical dimensions of the subject material. Evidence of original thinking and analysis will be apparent. In work of this standard, clear relationships between the topic and the wider context of the discipline will be drawn. Citation to the body of extant literature will be of a high standard.
Upper Second Class Honours	Grade B	60–69%	Work shows a good level of knowledge and analysis with critical appraisal of key issues supported by appropriate reference to the literature. It contains sophisticated argument and logical appraisal presented to a high standard.
Lower Second Class Honours	Grade C	50–59%	Work shows sound knowledge of subject material. Written response demonstrates an imbalance in favour of description rather than deeper critical thinking. Although some analysis present, this lacks sophistication.
Third Class Honours	Grade D	40–49%	Work shows limited evidence of knowledge and understanding of the subject material. Lack of analysis and evaluation of information and evidence. Reliance on reiteration of factual material and descriptive or narrative presentation of answer.
Fail	Grade F	35–39%	Work shows inadequate understanding of the task. Lack of coherent argument supported by use and interpretation of evidence drawn from the relevant literature.
Clear Fail	Ungraded	0–34%	Work shows little knowledge of the subject and no application to set task. Weak or no argument constructed. Plagiarism may be evident. Weak expression and use of language relevant to the discipline.

- **What is anonymous marking?** To ensure further that there is no bias in assessment, anonymous marking is often used. This means that the identity of the student is masked, possibly by use of Personal Identification or Matriculation numbers. Thus, your identity as creator of the text is unknown to the marker so that gender, ethnicity, age or academic record cannot influence the grading. However, the identity of the marker will normally be identified to you on the feedback sheet or note at the end of your text.

- **What do grades mean?** Each university sets its own grading scheme although these are broadly based on what is called the 'Honours Classification', that is, the division of degrees into First Class, Upper Second Class, Lower Second Class and Third Class. At lower levels of study, these classifications do not generally apply. However, the reality is that students and staff tend to think of work as falling within these categories. Tables 2.1 and 2.2 show some different versions of the scales that are used to grade students' work in terms of the Honours Classification.

Table 2.2 **Alpha-numeric marking scale, with corresponding aggregation scale used when combining elements of assessment.**

Descriptor	Reporting Scale	Aggregation Scale	Corresponding Honours classification
Excellent	A1 A2 A3	21 20 19	First Class
Very good	B1 B2 B3	18 17 16	Upper Second Class (2.1)
Good	C1 C2 C3	15 14 13	Lower Second Class (2.2)
Satisfactory	D1 D2 D3	12 11 10	Third Class
Marginal fail	MF	9	Marginal fail
Clear fail	CF	6	Clear fail
Bad fail	BF	2 0	Bad fail

→ What markers are looking for in terms of presentation

Lecturers frequently mark reading multiple responses to a set assignment and there is a considerable volume of reading involved in order to assess these. Therefore, assignments where ideas are expressed clearly in good prose tend to be viewed more favourably than those that are not. Submissions that make it difficult to follow the writer's train of thought are often those where the writing style is unclear for a variety of grammatical reasons. This can be attributed to sloppy editing and/or proof-reading. To help you to become more aware of the aspects you should be paying attention to, the checklist in Column 1 of Table 2.3 shows some of the presentational features taken into account in the assessment of essay work and this is also considered in **Ch 19**.

Presentation, structure and content

These three elements are interdependent, but experience suggests that presentation can act as a barrier to understanding and can lose you marks. If readers cannot read the document because of poor layout or language use, for example, then they will struggle to follow the structure of the document and any argument it might contain. Similarly, if the structure is also poorly framed and thus unclear, then the content is going to be difficult to recognise. It is for these reasons that presentation, structure and content are listed in that order.

Features of writing that can obstruct the understanding of the reader (the marker)

- Cliché (**Ch 10**)
- Colloquial language (**Ch 10**)
- Subjectivity (**Ch 10**)
- Poor sentence structure (**Ch 11**)
- Lack of agreement (**Ch 12**)
- Mixed-up tenses (**Ch 10** and **Ch 12**)
- Weak punctuation (**Ch 13**)
- Bad spelling (**Ch 14**)

→ What markers are looking for in terms of structure

The structure of a piece of writing is important both to convey your understanding of the issues related to the topic and to outline your response to the aspect that you have been asked to consider. Structure is created at sentence, paragraph and text level. Thus, it is important not only to ensure that sentences are concise and well structured, but also that paragraphs are coherent and well ordered.

While it may seem to be stating the obvious, an essay with an identifiable and coherent introduction will help the reader to understand the structure of the writing that follows, and so will attract a higher mark. Markers will also respond positively to a main body where the points are signposted clearly: for example, guiding the reader through the logic of causal relationships, analysis of a problem, or comparisons and contrasts. If this is followed by a tightly summarised analytical conclusion, then the marker is in a good position to assess the overall construction of the argument and more likely to reach a positive evaluation.

The checklist in Column 2 of Table 2.3 shows some of the structural considerations taken into account in marking criteria for essay work. **Ch 8** and **Ch 9** present structural models, and **Ch 11** explains how to create effective sentences and paragraphs.

→ What markers are looking for in terms of content

While markers are looking for factual knowledge and understanding of concepts, they do not want to read a list of facts. Rather, they would prefer to see how you can arrange these facts and concepts into structuring a response to the task you have been set.

Thus, markers want to be able to evaluate the writer's ability to think critically. To demonstrate this, the content of your essay has to show analysis of evidence that supports your case. It should not be simply a description or narrative based on lecture notes or information gathered from the Internet, but an evaluation of knowledge, showing deeper-level understanding in the context of the question that has been set. Moreover, at university level, you need to support your analysis with

Table 2.3 Checklist for essay writing in relation to typical marking criteria

Presentation	Structure	Content
□ **Writing style:** should be • objective; • formal as appropriate to academic writing; and • clear, correct, standard English with no truncated text messaging or other inappropriate abbreviations.	□ **Logic of writing:** your essay should be planned carefully so it has a logical structure. The construction of sentences and paragraphs should contribute to the overall cohesion of the text. Poorly constructed sentence-level errors will make the text difficult to understand and may hamper the reader's comprehension.	□ **Quality of knowledge:** Your essay should reflect • an understanding of the range of module/course themes and your ability to make connections across topics; and • reading from source material in addition to that presented in lectures.
□ **Printed format:** practice varies from institution to institution, but, generally, work is word-processed and printed. You need to follow standard typing conventions such as spacing, justification and punctuation. If work is handwritten, print neatly and never use capitals throughout.	□ **Logic of discussion or argument:** evidence should be organised in support of viewpoint but expressed in ways that avoid making value judgements (p. 80).	□ **Relevance:** the text should relate to the aspect of the topic defined by the task brief. If you write too much general material and fail to tackle the deeper, more complex, issues, then this will have a negative impact on your grade.

□ **Spellcheck:** word processor spellchecking functions are not foolproof, so you also need to read your work over, paying particular attention, for example, to words that sound the same but have different spelling or words that are specific to your subject and that may have been misspelt in the text.

□ **Grammar check:** your word-processor may indicate 'errors' of grammar (as well as misspelling) by underlining them. Check each of these, but note that often the diagnosed 'errors' are simply suggestions for you to consider in context. For example, use of the passive is often highlighted and acceptable in academic writing and thus alteration may be unnecessary.

□ **Relationship to literature:** in many disciplines, the line of argument that you need to construct should relate to key works in existing literature. You will be given credit for making these connections within your text, being careful, of course, to avoid plagiarism. If you fail to make these links or fail to explain why you are making them, then your work is weakened.

□ **Use of tables, diagrams, graphs or figures:** some subjects routinely require evidence to be presented in a visual format. If you need to demonstrate evidence in this way, ensure that visuals are labelled appropriately and are integrated into the text in a logical manner close to the text that explains their content. This contributes to the cohesion of your argument and the structure of your text.

□ **Critical thinking:** your essay must demonstrate an ability to analyse and synthesise complex ideas; and, at higher levels of study, demonstrate some ability to construct an original argument.

□ **Use of primary sources:** in some subjects the ability to analyse and evaluate material from primary sources will set your work apart from that of others as significant and worthy of a higher grade.

citations from a variety of primary and secondary sources using a recognised citation and referencing system (**Ch 18**). This helps you to show evidence of your study of the subject and demonstrates that you have embedded your answer within the wider context of your subject area.

However, if your use of this material relies too heavily on direct quotation or simply reformulates the wording by changing a few words from the original text, then you will not gain marks. Thus, it is vital that you paraphrase the ideas of others and use them to good purpose to support your response to the task and not merely to 'name-drop' in the text so that you can provide a lengthy reference list.

The checklist in Column 3 of Table 2.3 shows some of the content elements that are taken into account in the assessment of essay work. **Ch 7** addresses critical thinking, and **Ch 17** and **Ch 18** the rationale and methods for citing source material.

→ How essay feedback can help you to improve your future grades

Feedback from your lecturers should indicate where you can improve your written work for subsequent assignments and exams (see **Ch 20**). If the comments are unclear, or you cannot understand why you received the grade you did, then ask the marker or another tutor to provide additional comments. Most will respond helpfully to a polite request. You should use this information to create an action plan for enhancing the quality of your future work. This might involve consulting and acting on some of the material in later chapters of this book, for example.

---

smart tip

Developing proof-reading strategies

The ability to read your own written work critically is vital if you aspire to high standards.

- For coursework, editing your own essay drafts may be part of a developmental process leading to a finished product of high quality (see **Ch 16**).

- In exams, you should allocate some time for rereading essay answers so that you can weed out obvious mistakes and make quick additions where required – this may gain you valuable marks (see **Ch 21**).

Presentation

- **Find out whether sub-headings are acceptable in your subject.** If they are allowed, then they will act as useful pointers to structure and content and help you to organise your thoughts and writing. If not, consider using them at draft level, then remove them prior to submission.

- **Create a glossary.** Compile a glossary of subject-specific terms that will probably be used in your essay and refer to this as you write to ensure that you are not guilty of misspelling or misuse of jargon.

Structure

- **Plan the structure of your essay.** Avoid a 'stream of consciousness' approach that results in a paper that rambles and has no particular structure.

- **Focus on relevance.** Make sure that the paper you write is an appropriate response to the task that was set.

- **Ensure you analyse rather than describe.** For example, avoid simplistic chronological descriptions that do not contribute to a critical analysis of the topic.

- **Use signpost words.** These can be used to considerable effect in providing a logical path through your work to ensure that the marker is able to follow your thought process.

Content

- **Ensure that your work is factually correct.** Carelessness in this respect will lose you marks.

- **Interpret the subject for yourself.** In most cases, the marker is looking for *your* analysis and not a replication of any viewpoint that you perceive might have been held by the lecturer. It is worth remembering that, in many subjects, there are no 'right' answers, only good ones. As long as your answer is well constructed and well argued with supporting evidence from the literature, and not a hotchpotch reiteration of what you heard in a lecture or gleaned from handouts, then it will be judged favourably on those merits.

GO And now . . .

2.1 Find out more about grading scales and marking criteria for your university or department/school. These should be published online or as hard copy in handbooks. Reflect on your recent grades and identify ways in which you could improve them in the light of this information and the degree classification you aim to achieve.

2.2 Construct plans for essay-type assignments. In preparing your next assignment, ensure that you deconstruct and interpret the assignment task carefully, and that you construct a plan that reflects the thought process of your analysis and which you can then mould into a structured piece of writing.

2.3 Review a piece of writing that has been assessed by one of your lecturers. Read the feedback and note any points that might apply to your later assignments in relation to presentation, structure and content. Ensure that you act on these modifications in your next submission.

Getting started

3 Tackling writing assignments

How to get started

Assignments at university challenge you to write in different forms. This chapter looks at the fundamental stages in preparing to respond to any assignment. It takes you through a step-by-step process to help you plan the structure of your submission.

Key topics:

→ Realistic time planning
→ Recognising the elements of the task
→ Exploring the topic
→ Finding the material and selecting what's relevant
→ Adopting an analytical approach

Key terms
Analyse   Argue   Describe   Restriction   Topic

Written university assignments take different forms. Examples include essays, reports, project dossiers, short-answer mini-essays, case studies or dissertations. The purpose is to give you an opportunity to demonstrate several things:

- your knowledge and understanding of a topic;
- your ability to research a specific aspect of the topic set in the assignment; and
- your ability to organise supporting information and evidence within a structured piece of academic writing.

Especially for a longer piece of writing, or one that will count towards a module or degree mark, it is worth planning your work carefully to ensure that you approach the task in a focused manner.

→ Realistic time planning

Consult the course handbook for the assignment submission date. Work out how long you have between the starting point and due date, and then work out how much of that time you can devote to completion of the work. Remember to take into account things you may need to do for other subjects, your need to attend lectures, tutorials or practicals, and any family or part-time work commitments. Next, divide the available time into convenient working periods, decide how much time you wish to allocate to each aspect of the task and map these time allowances onto the available time (Table 3.1).

Value of planning

Time spent deconstructing the task and planning your response will enable you to save time in the long run and, as with most jobs, the quality of the preparation will be reflected in the quality of the end product. It is well worth taking time to break down the question into its different elements (see opposite). Good planning ensures that you can realistically complete the work before the submission date. It also allows you to balance the time spent on different components, devote sufficient time to aspects such as editing and proof-reading and avoid penalties that might be imposed because of late submission.

Table 3.1 **Subdivisions of a large writing task and their estimated timing.** A possible method of organising your time when planning a lengthy written assignment.

Aspect of task	Time allocated	When I plan to do this
Analysing the task		
Doing preliminary reading		
Planning the response to the task		
Doing supplementary reading		
Writing the first draft		
Reviewing the first draft		
Editing/proof-reading the final copy		
Printing/writing out the final copy		
Time margin for the unexpected		

Once you have thought about the amount of time you can allocate to the work, the next phase of analysing an assignment requires you to break the task down into its component parts by asking yourself the following questions:

- **What's the *instruction*?** Many assignments are not in the form of questions but framed as commands introduced by an instruction word. It is important to interpret these instruction words properly.
- **What's the *topic*?** This will clarify the context of the discussion you will need to construct.
- **What's the *aspect* of the topic?** This will help you define a more specific focus within the wider context.
- **What *restriction* is imposed on the topic?** This will limit the scope of your discussion.

The example below shows you how this analysis might look for a sample question.

Example assignment analysis

Task: 'Assess the importance of post-operative care in the rehabilitation of orthopaedic patients'.

Instruction: assess.

Topic: post-operative care.

Aspect: importance.

Restriction 1: rehabilitation.

Restriction 2: orthopaedic patients.

You may already deconstruct questions, topics, assignments and other tasks in this way subconsciously, but there is value in marking these elements out on paper. First, it helps you to recognise the scope and limitations of the work you have been asked to complete. Second, it reduces the risk of producing a piece of work that waffles or strays from the point. Once you have gone through this fairly quick process, you will be better able to work on planning your writing and on adopting a suitable framework for your assignment.

Table 3.2 shows a range of typical instruction words, with definitions for each one. You should make sure you know what's expected of you when any of these instructions are used, not only in terms of these definitions, but also in relation to the thinking processes expected (**Ch 7**). However, always remember to take the whole question into account when deciding this.

Generally, instruction words fall into four categories, although this grouping may vary according to the context of the question. The list below defines these types. In broad terms, this suggests differences in the approach you can take to tackling assignments that will dictate how you need to organise the information in your assignment.

Instruction word categories

One way of categorising instruction words is by looking at what they ask you to do:

Do: create something, draw up a plan, calculate.

Describe: explain or show how something appears, happens or works.

Analyse: look at all sides of an issue.

Argue: look at all sides of an issue and provide supporting evidence for your position.

→ Exploring the topic

Go back to the task and analyse the topic, its aspect(s) and restriction(s) more deeply. This is important because students often misread the task and, although they may submit a good piece of work, their response may miss the focus of the assignment.

Next, create a concept 'map' of the topic by writing down as many related aspects as you can in a free-flowing diagram (see Figure 6.5). Revisit the instruction word and consider how this applies to your initial response to the task. This may seem to be a strange approach, but these immediate thoughts are principally your own 'take' on the topic, perhaps influenced by lectures, but before you have been influenced by any reading material. The most important aspect is that you are beginning to exercise your critical thinking skills, by analysing for yourself what you think is important about this subject.

Table 3.2 Instruction words for assignments and exams. These words are the product of research into the frequency of use of the most common instruction words in university examinations. The definitions below are suggestions: you must take the whole question into account when answering. See also Table 7.1.

Instruction word	Definition - what you are expected to do
Account [give an]	Describe
Account for	Give reasons for
Analyse	Give an organised answer looking at all aspects
Apply	Put a theory into operation
Assess	Decide on value/importance
Brief account [give a]	Describe in a concise way
Comment on	Give your opinion
Compare [with]	Discuss similarities; draw conclusions on common areas
Compile	Make up (a list/plan/outline)
Consider	Describe/give your views on the subject
Contrast	Discuss differences/draw own view
Criticise	Point out weak/strong points, i.e. give a balanced answer
Define	Give the meaning of a term, concisely
Demonstrate	Show by example/evidence
Describe	Narrative on process/appearance/operation/sequence . . .
Devise	Make up
Discuss	Give own thoughts and support your opinion or conclusion
Evaluate	Decide on merit of situation/argument
Exemplify	Show by giving examples
Expand	Give more information
Explain	Give reason for/say why
Explain how	Describe how something works
Identify	Pinpoint/list
Illustrate	Give examples
Indicate	Point out, but not in great detail
Justify	Support the argument for . . .
List	Make an organised list, e.g. events, components, aspects
Outline	Describe basic factors/limited information
Plan	Think how to organise something
Report	Give an account of the process or event
Review	Write a report/give facts and views on facts
Show	Demonstrate with supporting evidence
Specify	Give details of something
State	Give a clear account of . . .
Summarise	Briefly give an account
Trace	Provide a brief chronology of events/process
Work out	Find a solution, e.g. as in a maths problem

Brainstorming techniques

To create an effective concept 'map', use a single sheet of A4 in the landscape position. This gives more space for lateral thinking and creativity. It also leaves more space for additions to be made at later stages. Figure 6.5 illustrates how to do this.

→ Finding the material and selecting what's relevant

As a preliminary to tackling the prescribed reading list or delving into the literature, you may find it useful to obtain some general background information about the topic. Typical additional sources you could consider are shown below.

Reading the literature that supports a subject is a routine part of student activity. Generally, reading lists are extensive to give some choice; they often list basic texts and then sources that go into greater depth. It is not usually expected that you read everything on these lists. In some subjects, you may only be expected to look at

Sources of information

Handouts/PowerPoint slides: should outline key issues and ideas, pose problems and provide solutions related to your topic.

Lecture notes: present an analysis of a topic; easy to locate if you've noted lecturer, topic and date.

General or subject encyclopaedias: provide a thumb-nail sketch of useful background information; give key points to direct your reading in more detailed texts. Electronic versions may be available through your university library.

Library resources: the electronic catalogue will enable you to locate many useful resources (**Ch 5**). You may also find things serendipitously by browsing in the relevant zone of shelving in the library, where it is possible to find books and journals that may not necessarily come up from the search headings you have selected when consulting the catalogue. E-resources, such as ebrary and e-journals may also be accessed via your library's website.

one or two recommended texts. In some other subjects, book lists are lengthy and the volume of reading may seem daunting, but the task will be more manageable if you approach it systematically.

Unless specific chapters or pages are cited, students sometimes think that they need to read the whole book. This is usually not the case. Use the contents page and the index in partnership to identify which sections are relevant to your topic. Some authors put key pages in bold type in the index and this will help you to focus your reading on a specific topic. At this stage also, preliminary encyclopaedia reading may help you to identify sections in a book resource that are more relevant to the present task.

Begin by doing the necessary reading and note-making. This has to be focused and you need to be reading with discrimination (**Ch 4**). As you move from basic texts to more specialised books or journal articles that give more detailed analysis, your understanding of the topic will deepen. This may mean, for example, that you begin to build up a more informed picture of events, implications of a procedure or the possible solutions to a problem. What are you looking for? For instance, this could be facts, examples, information to support a particular viewpoint, or counter-arguments to provide balance to your analysis of the topic. As you become more familiar with the issues, the easier it will be to think critically about what you are reading (**Ch 7**) and consequently build your response to the task you have been set. Continue to add to your initial brainstorm.

smart tip

The reporter's questions

Sometimes it is difficult to distinguish the important from the unimportant, the relevant from the irrelevant. A well-tried strategy, applicable in many subjects, is to ask yourself the questions that a trainee journalist is advised to use:

- **Who?** Who is involved in relation to this topic, for example, which people/organisations?
- **What?** What are the problems/issues involved?
- **When?** What is the time-frame to be considered?
- **Where?** Where did it occur?
- **Why?** What reasons are relevant to this issue/topic?
- **How?** How has this situation been reached?

→ Adopting an analytical approach

Knowing what information to put aside and what to retain requires a more disciplined appraisal than the more wide-ranging approach you will have followed in your initial reading. Asking certain questions may help you to focus on what is important to your topic. For example:

● Who are the key actors in a sequence of events?
● What are the important or necessary factors that explain particular situations?
● What explanations support a particular view?
● What patterns can be identified, for example, short-, medium- and long-term factors?

From your reading and note-making you will begin to find that different authors make similar or contradictory points. As you begin to identify the different schools of thought or approaches to an issue, you should begin to cross-reference your notes so that you can group authors who subscribe to the same or similar viewpoints.

---

smart tip

Direct quotation

It is important not to rely too heavily on quoting from the text. Firstly, if this is overdone, then it is plagiarism (**Ch 17**); secondly, it fails to give evidence that you understand the significance of the point being made.

University work needs more than simple reproduction of facts. You need to be able to construct an argument and to support this with evidence. This means that you need to draw on the literature that you have read in order to support your position. In some instances, dependent on the topic and discipline, it may be appropriate to present differing viewpoints and evaluate arguments one over the others, and, if appropriate, address counter-arguments to these. What is important is to present a tight, well-argued case for the view you finally present as the one you favour.

Once you have evolved your own response to the task you have been set, you then need to place this within a framework that presents your response in a way that is well structured (**Ch 8** and **Ch 9**). Writing that follows a sequence of sound logic and argument will improve your potential for gaining better marks.

Practical tips for getting started on a writing assignment

Explore the full range of available material. In the early years of university study many students follow the same practices as they used at school, often with too much reliance on handouts and notes from a single core textbook. At university you will be expected to read more widely by identifying source material beyond titles given as a basic starting point. It is worthwhile exploring your library on foot to browse in the areas related to your studies, where you may find a whole range of material that potentially expands your reading and understanding.

Spend time reading. This is a vital part of the writing process, but you should recognise the dangers of prolonging the reading phase beyond your scheduled deadline (**Ch 9**). This is an avoidance strategy that is quite common. Students may delay getting down to planning the structure and moving on to the writing phase because they are uncomfortable with writing. Facing up to these next phases and getting on with them is usually much less formidable once you get started, so it's best to stick to your time plan for this assignment and move on to the next phase in the planned sequence.

Keep records of your reading. It is exasperating to know that you have read something somewhere but cannot find it again. It is good to develop the habit of noting page number, chapter, title, author, publisher and place of publication on notes you make. This makes citation and referencing much easier and less time-consuming (**Ch 18**).

Conserve material. In the process of marshalling information for a writing task you will probably obtain some interesting and potentially useful material that proves to be irrelevant to the current writing task. It is well worth keeping this in your filing system because this topic may come up again at a later date in a subtle way. In exam revision, this personal cache of information could be useful in revitalising your knowledge and understanding of this topic.

(GO) And now . . .

3.1 Practise categorising instruction words. Go to Table 3.2 and mark out all those instruction words that would invite a response asking you to *do something practical*, those requiring you simply to *describe*, those that invite you to *analyse* and those that are directing you to *construct an argument*.

3.2 Examine some of the assignment titles that you will have to complete in a selected subject. Taking the whole question or instruction into account, identify what type of approach is needed - doing something practical, describing, analysing or arguing. You may find that within the same question/task you will have to do some describing in order to analyse or argue. The trick generally is not to devote too much time to the descriptive element at the expense of analysis/argument. You could also do this activity with past exam papers.

3.3 Try creating the wording for a task in a selected subject for yourself. Think about the clarity of the question. Is it ambiguous? Is it unclear? Identify your topic, aspect and restriction(s). Turning the student-examiner roles around can sometimes be a helpful way of developing your understanding. This could be an excellent preparation for exams because it helps with anticipating possible questions and reflecting on how you would answer them. This broadens the range of possible questions you could feel comfortable tackling in exams.

Researching your topic

4 | Effective academic reading

How to read efficiently and with understanding

Whatever your discipline, you will find that you are required to do a lot of reading when preparing to write an essay or assignment. This chapter explains how to develop the speed-reading skills that will help you to deal more effectively with academic text.

Key topics:
→ Surveying the overall organisation of the text
→ How to examine the structure of the writing itself
→ Speed-reading techniques

Key terms
Blurb   Finger tracing   Gist   Terminator paragraph   Topic paragraph
Topic sentence

Much of the material you will read as part of your studies will be books and journal articles ('papers') written following traditional academic style, and may appear, at first glance, to be heavy going. However, by taking advantage of the way printed academic resources are organised and understanding how text within them is structured, you should find it easier to read the pages of print in a way that will help you gain an understanding of the content while saving you time.

→ Surveying the overall organisation of the text

A text may be suggested by tutors; alternatively, when expanding your lecture notes or revising, you may come across another resource that looks as if it might be relevant. In either case, carry out a preliminary survey to familiarise yourself with what it contains. You can use elements of the structure to answer key questions about the content, as follows:

Reading and note-making

This chapter is concerned mainly with reading and comprehension as a prelude to note-making. While it is possible to read and make notes at the same time, this is not always the most effective form of studying, as your notes may end up simply as a rewrite of the source text. Notes framed after you have scanned the prescribed section of text will be better if you have a clearer idea of their context and content.

- **Title and author(s).** Does this text or paper look as though it is going to be useful to your current task? Are the authors well-known authorities in the subject area?
- **Publisher's 'blurb' or abstract.** Does this indicate that the coverage suits your needs?
- **Publication details.** What is the date of publication? Will this book provide you with up-to-date coverage? Is this the most recent edition?
- **Contents listing (for books and reviews).** Does this indicate that the resource covers the key topic areas you need? Do the chapter/section titles suggest the coverage is detailed enough?
- **Index (for books).** Is this comprehensive and will it help you find what you want, quickly? From a quick look, can you see references to material you want?

What is your reading goal?

It is always a good idea to decide this before you start reading any piece of text.

- If you are looking for a specific point of information, then this can often be done quickly, using the index or chapter titles as a guide.
- If you wish to expand your lecture notes using a textbook, then you might read in a different way, which might result in note-making.
- If your aim is to appreciate the author's style or the aesthetics of a piece of writing, perhaps in a work of fiction, then you may read more slowly and reread key parts.

Sometimes, different methods may be required, for example, in English literature, 'close reading' techniques. These specialised methods will probably be taught as part of your studies.

- **General impression.** Does the text look easy to read? Is the text easy to navigate via sub-headings? Is any visual material clear and explained well?

The answers to these questions will help you to decide whether to investigate further; whether you need to look at the whole resource, or just selected parts; or whether the book or article is of limited value at the present time.

→ How to examine the structure of the writing itself

Well-structured academic text usually follows a standard pattern with an introduction, main body and conclusion in each element. Sometimes the introduction may comprise several paragraphs; sometimes it may be only one paragraph. Similarly, the conclusion may be several paragraphs or only one. Figure 4.1 shows a layout for a piece of text with five paragraphs, comprising an introduction and conclusion with three intervening paragraphs of varying length.

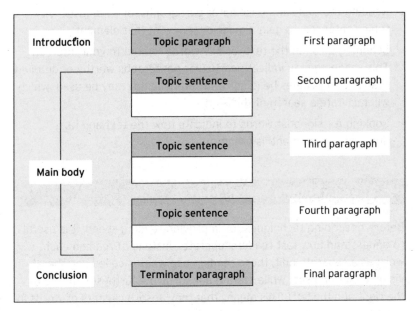

Figure 4.1 Sample textual layout. You can visualise the structure of any piece of reading material in a similar fashion.

Reader as author

The points in this chapter about the organisation of printed material and the structure of text are important for you as a reader or decoder of text, and they also come into play when you become an academic author and have to put your own ideas clearly – they help your reader (often 'the marker') to decode your written text.

Within the structure of the text, each paragraph will be introduced by a topic sentence stating the content of the paragraph. Each paragraph performs a function. For example, some may describe, others may provide examples, while others may examine points in favour of a particular viewpoint and others points against that viewpoint.

The function of these paragraphs, and the sentences within them, is usually signalled by use of 'signpost words', which guide the reader through the logical structure of the text. For example, the word 'however' indicates that some contrast is about to be made with a point immediately before; 'therefore' or 'thus' signal that a result or effect is about to be explained. You can use this knowledge of the structure of writing to establish the substance of a piece of text by:

- Reading the topic and terminator paragraphs, or even just their topic sentences, to gain a quick overview of that element.
- Scanning through the text for key words related to your interest. This scanning may indicate particular paragraphs worthy of detailed reading. Sometimes headings and sub-headings may be used, which will facilitate a search of this kind.
- Looking for signpost words to indicate how the text and its underlying 'argument' is organised.

→ Speed-reading techniques

Before describing techniques for improving reading speed, it is useful to understand how fast readers 'operate'. Instead of reading each word as a separate unit, these readers use what is called peripheral vision (what you see, while staring ahead, at the furthest extreme to the right and the left). This means that they absorb clusters of words in one 'flash' or 'fixation' on the text, as shown in Figure 4.2(a). In this example, four fixations are required to read that single line of text.

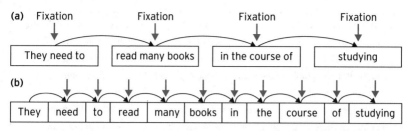

Figure 4.2 **Eye movements when reading.** (a) Reader who makes eye fixations on clusters of words. (b) Reader who reads every word one by one.

A reader who does this is reading more efficiently than the reader who reads word by word (Figure 4.2(b)). This reader makes 12 fixations along the line, which means that their reading efficiency is low. Research has also indicated that people who read slowly in this way are less likely to absorb information quickly enough for the brain to comprehend. Therefore, reading slowly can actually hinder comprehension rather than assist it.

As a practised reader, you will probably have developed these fast-reading skills to some degree. They can be improved using techniques like the 'eye gymnastics' exercise in Figure 4.3. Other things you can do include 'finger tracing', where you run your finger below the line of text being read to follow your eyes' path across a page, starting and stopping a word or two from either side. This is said to increase your eye speed, keep your mind focused on the words being read and prevent you from skipping back to previous sentences or jumping forward to text that follows. Some people find it helpful to use a bookmark placed horizontally along the line they are reading, because it makes a useful guide that prevents the eye jumping ahead of the text they are reading.

Origin of speed-reading

The basic techniques were developed in the 1950s by Evelyn Wood, an American educator. She set up institutes to teach students to develop an ability to read hundreds of words per minute. Those who have studied her method include businessmen and politicians, who have to learn to read lengthy papers quickly but with understanding. US Presidents Jimmy Carter and John F. Kennedy were both regarded as famous speed-reading practitioners.

Learning to read quickly	is a skill	that needs to be developed.
If you have to read	a new piece of text,	you will find it useful
first of all	to read	the first paragraph
and the last paragraph	of the section, chapter or article.	From this
you should be able	to gauge	the context
and general outline	of the topic under discussion.	While it is true
that all academic texts	should have been well edited	before publication,
it does not follow	that every text	will follow these conventions.
However,	a well-written piece	of academic writing
should follow this pattern	and, as a reader,	you should exploit
this convention	in order to help you	to understand
the overall content	before you embark	on intensive reading
of the text.		

When you are about to	make notes from texts	you should not begin
by sitting	with notepad ready	and the pen poised.
Certainly	make a note of	publication details needed
for your bibliography,	but resist the temptation	to start taking notes
at the same time as	beginning	your first reading of the text.
It is better	to read first,	reflect, recall
and then write notes	based on	what you remember.
This gives you	a framework	around which
you ought to be able	to organise your notes	after you have read
the text intensively.	People who start	by writing notes
as soon as	they open the book	will end up
copying	more and more from the text	as their tiredness increases.
In this case	very little	reflection or learning
is achieved.		

Figure 4.3 'Eye gymnastics' exercise. Try to read the above text quite quickly. Read from left to right in the normal way. The aim of the activity is to train your eyes to make more use of your peripheral vision when you are reading. In this way, you will learn to make fewer fixations on the text by forcing your eyes to focus on the centre of a group of words, which are printed in naturally occurring clusters – usually on the basis of grammatical or logical framing. It may be that you experience some discomfort behind your eyes, which indicates that they are adjusting to this less familiar pattern. If this is the case, you should keep practising using this text as a means of developing the speed of your eye movements.

Things that can reduce your reading speed

As well as trying methods to read faster, you should be aware of
circumstances that might slow you down. These include:

- distractions such as background noise of television, music or
  chatter;
- sub-vocalisation (sounding out each word aloud as it is read);
- reading word by word;
- over-tiredness;
- poor eyesight – if you think your eyes are not 20:20, then it might
  be worth going for an eye test; your eyes are too important to
  neglect and a pair of reading glasses may make a huge difference
  to your studying comfort;
- poor lighting – if you can, read using a lamp that can shine
  directly on to the text; reading in poor light causes eye strain
  and this, in turn, limits concentration and the length of reading
  episodes.

Increasing your reading speed using finger tracing

Try the following method:

- Select a reading passage of about two pages in length (you
  could use the sample text in Table 4.1). Note your starting and
  finishing time and calculate your reading speed using Method B
  in Table 4.2.
- Take a break of 40–60 minutes.
- Return to the text and run a finger along the line of text much
  faster than you could possibly read it.
- Repeat, but more slowly, so that you can just read it ('finger
  tracing'). Again, note your starting and finishing times, and work
  out your reading speed. You should find that your reading speed
  has increased from the first reading.
- Carry out this exercise at the same time of day over a week, using
  texts of similar length and complexity to help you increase your
  reading speed.

Table 4.1 Sample reading text, showing reading 'signposts'. This text might represent the introduction to a textbook on modern communications in electrical engineering, journalism, marketing or psychology. The light shaded areas indicate the topic sentences; darker shading indicates the signpost words. You can also use this text of 744 words to assess your speed of reading (see Table 4.2).

Introduction Topic paragraph	Technological advances and skilful marketing have meant that the mobile phone has moved from being simply an accessory to a status as an essential piece of equipment. From teenagers to grandmothers, the nation has taken to the mobile phone as a constant link for business and social purposes. As a phenomenon, the ascendancy of the mobile phone, in a multitude of ways, has had a critical impact on the way people organise their lives.	Topic sentence
	Clearly, the convenience of the mobile is attractive. It is constantly available to receive or send calls. While these are not cheap, the less expensive text-message alternative provides a similar 'constant contact' facility. At a personal and social level, this brings peace of mind to parents as teenagers can locate and be located on the press of a button. However, in business terms, while it means that employees are constantly accessible and, with more sophisticated models, can access internet communications also, there is no escape from the workplace.	Topic sentence Signpost word Signpost word
	The emergence of abbreviated text-message language has wrought a change in everyday print. For example, pupils and students have been known to submit written work using text message symbols and language. Some have declared this to mark the demise of standard English. Furthermore, the accessibility of the mobile phone has become a problem in colleges and universities where it has been known for students in examinations to use the texting facility to obtain information required.	Topic sentence Signpost word Signpost word
	The ubiquity of the mobile phone has generated changes in the way that services are offered. For instance, this means that trains, buses, and restaurants have declared 'silent zones' where the mobile is not permitted, to give others a rest from the 'I'm on the train' style mobile phone conversation.	Topic sentence Signpost words
Transition paragraph	While the marked increase in mobile phone sales indicates that many in the population have embraced this technology, by contrast, 'mobile' culture has not been without its critics. Real concerns have been expressed about the potential dangers that can be encountered through mobile phone use.	Topic sentence Signpost words

Table 4.1 continued

	One such danger is that associated with driving while speaking on a mobile. A body of case law has been accumulated to support the introduction of new legislation outlawing the use of hand-held mobile phones by drivers while driving. The enforcement of this legislation is virtually impossible to police and, thus, much is down to the common sense and responsibility of drivers. Again, technology has risen to meet the contingency with the development of 'hands-free' phones that can be used while driving and without infringing the law.	Topic sentence Signpost word
	A further danger is an unseen one, namely the impact of the radiation from mobile phones on the human brain. Research is not well advanced in this area and data related to specific absorption rates (SARs) from the use of mobile phones and its effect on brain tissue is not yet available for evaluation. Nevertheless, although this lack of evidence is acknowledged by mobile phone companies, they advise that hands-free devices reduce the SARs levels by 98 per cent.	Topic sentence Signpost word
	Mobile phone controversy is not confined only to the potential dangers related to the units alone; some people have serious concerns about the impact mobile phone masts have on the area surrounding them. The fear is that radiation from masts could induce serious illness among those living near such masts. While evidence refuting or supporting this view remains inconclusive, there appears to be much more justification for concern about emissions from television transmitters and national grid pylons, which emit far higher levels of electro-magnetic radiation. Yet, little correlation appears to have been made between this fundamental of electrical engineering and the technology of telecommunications.	Topic sentence Signpost word Signpost word
Conclusion Terminator paragraph	In summary, although it appears that there are enormous benefits to mobile phone users, it is clear that there are many unanswered questions about the impact of their use on individuals. At one level, these represent an intrusion on personal privacy, whether as a user or as a bystander obliged to listen to multiple one-sided conversations in public places. More significantly, there is the potential for unseen damage to the health of individual users as they clamp their mobiles to their ears. Whereas the individual has a choice to use or not to use a mobile phone, people have fewer choices in relation to exposure to dangerous emissions from masts. While the output from phone masts is worthy of further investigation, it is in the more general context of emissions from electro-magnetic masts of all types that serious research needs to be developed.	Topic sentence Signpost words Signpost words Signpost word Signpost word

Table 4.2 **How to calculate your reading speed.** These two examples show the principles of how to do this calculation.

Method A (specified reading time)	
a Select a chapter from a textbook (this is better than a newspaper or journal article because these are often printed in columns)	
b Calculate the average number of words per line, e.g. 50 words counted over 5 lines	= 10 words per line
c Count the number of lines per page	= 41 total lines
d Multiply (b × c) = 10 × 41	= 410 words per page
e Read for a specific time (to the nearest minute or half-minute) without stopping	= 4 minutes' reading
f Number of pages read in 4 minutes	= 2.5 pages read
g Multiply (d × f) = 410 × 2.5	= 1025 total words read
h Divide (g ÷ e) = 1025 ÷ 4	= **256 words per minute**
Method B (specified text length)	
a Find a piece of text of known or estimated word length (see method A)	= 744 words
b Note the time taken to read this in seconds	= 170 seconds
c Convert the seconds to a decimal fraction of minutes = 170 ÷ 60	= 2.8 minutes
d Divide (a ÷ c) = 744 ÷ 2.8	= **266 words per minute**

The average reading speed is said to be 265 words per minute (wpm). Reading speed for university students may be slightly lower, as aspects like difficulty of the text, unfamiliarity with the terminology used and the complexity of the concepts being discussed in the text have the potential to slow down reading. However, as you become more familiar with the subject and the issues being covered in your course and, thus, with your supplementary reading, then your reading speed will increase.

You can assess your normal reading speed using either method described in Table 4.2. The text of Table 4.1 is a suitable piece of writing whose word length is already known, should you wish to try method B. If your reading speed seems slow, then you can work on improving it by using a similar level and length of text at the same time each day. Go through the reading speed process and, gradually, you should see your average creeping up.

There are many other strategies you can develop to read and absorb content quickly. These include:

- **Skimming.** Pick out a specific piece of information by quickly letting your eye run down a list or over a page looking for a key word or phrase, as when seeking a particular name or address in a phone book.

- **Scanning.** Let your eye run quickly over a chapter or article, for example, before you commit yourself to study-read the whole text. This will help you to gain an overview of the text before you start.

- **Picking out the topic sentences.** As seen in Figure 4.1 and Table 4.1, by reading the topic sentences you will be able to flesh out your overview of the text content. This will aid your understanding before you study-read the whole text.

- **Identifying the signpost words.** As noted above, these help guide you as the reader through the logical process that the author has mapped out for you.

- **Recognising clusters of grammatically allied words.** Subliminally, you will be grouping words in clusters according to their natural alliances (sometimes called 'collocation'). This will help you to read by making fewer fixations and this will improve your reading speed. You can improve your speed at doing this by using the eye-gymnastics exercise described earlier.

- **Taking cues from punctuation.** As you read, you will gain some understanding by interpreting the text using the cues of full stops and commas, for example, to help you gain understanding of what you are reading. The importance of punctuation to comprehension is vital.

To be effective, reading quickly must be matched by a good level of comprehension. Conversely, reading too slowly can mean that comprehension is hampered. Clearly, you need to incorporate tests of your understanding to check that you have understood the main points of the text. One method of reading that incorporates this is called the SQ3R method – survey, question, read, recall and review (Table 4.3). This is also a helpful strategy for exam revision as it incorporates the development of memory and learning skills simultaneously. Another test of assimilation is note-taking. This is covered in **Ch 6.**

Table 4.3 Reading for remembering and understanding: the SQ3R method.
The point of this method is that the reader has to engage in processing the material in the text and is not simply reading on 'autopilot' where very little is being retained.

Survey stage
• Read the first paragraph (topic paragraph) and last paragraph (terminator paragraph) of a chapter or page of notes • Read the topic sentences for each intervening paragraph • Focus on the headings and sub-headings, if present • Study the graphs and diagrams for key features
Question stage
• What do you know already about this topic? • What is the author likely to tell you? • What specifically do you need to find out?
Read stage
• Read the entire section *quickly* to get the gist of the piece of writing; finger-tracing techniques may be helpful at this point • Go back to the question stage and revisit your initial answers • Look especially for keywords, key statements, signpost words • Do *not* stop to look up unknown words – go for completion
Recall stage
• Turn the book or your notes over and try to recall as much as possible • Make key pattern headings/notes/diagrams/flow charts (**Ch 6**) • Turn over the book again • Check over for accuracy of recall; suggested recall periods – every 20 minutes
Review stage
• After a break, try to recall the main points

Practical tips for reading effectively and with understanding

Be selective and understand your purpose. Think about why you are reading. Look at the material you have already collected relating to the subject or topic you are writing about. For example, this should include lecture notes, which ought to remind you of the way a topic was presented, the thrust of an argument or a procedure. Are you reading to obtain a general overview or is it to identify additional specific information? Use a technique and material that suits your needs.

Adjust your reading speed according to the type of text you have to read. A marginally interesting article in a newspaper will probably require less intensive reading than a key chapter in an academic book.

Grasp the general message before dealing with difficult parts. Not all texts are 'reader friendly'. If you find a section of text difficult to understand, then skip over that bit; toiling over it will probably not increase your understanding. Continue with your reading and when you come to a natural break in the text, for example, the end of a chapter or section, then go back to the 'sticky' bit and reread it. Usually, second time round, it will make more sense because you have an overview of the context. Similarly, don't stop every time you come across a new word. Read on and try to get the gist of the meaning from the rest of the text. When you have finished, look the word up in a dictionary and add to your personal glossary.

Take regular breaks. Reading continuously over a long period of time is counterproductive. Concentration is at a peak after 20 minutes, but wanes after 40 minutes. Take regular breaks, making sure that your breaks do not become longer than your study stints.

Follow up references within your text. When you are reading, you need to be conscious of the citations to other authors that might be given in the text; not all will be relevant to your reading purpose, but it is worth quickly noting the ones that look most interesting as you come across them. You'll usually find the full publication details in the references at the end of the chapter/article or at the end of the book. This will give you sufficient information to supplement your reading once you have finished reading the 'parent' text.

GO And now . . .

4.1 Monitor your reading speed. Choose a suitable text and calculate your speed using either method A or B in Table 4.2. If you feel your speed is relatively slow, then try out some of the methods suggested in the speed-reading section of this chapter. After a period of using these methods, and deciding which suits you best, check your speed to see if you have improved.

▶

4.2 Practise surveying a text using a book from your reading list. Rather than simply opening your reading resource at the prescribed pages, spend five or ten minutes surveying the whole book. Think about how the author has organised the content and why. Keep this in mind when reading the text, and reflect on whether this has improved your comprehension and assimilation of the content.

4.3 Become more familiar with the reading cues embedded within texts. As shown within this chapter, conventions of grammar, punctuation and spelling are useful in providing clues to meaning for the reader. If you would like to look into these topics further, then see **Ch 12, Ch 13** and **Ch 14**.

5 | The library as a resource

How to make the best use of the facilities

When writing essays and other assignments you will be expected not only to seek out the books on your reading list, but also to source additional material for yourself. Learning more about your university library and how to access its resources is a priority. This chapter offers some suggestions and strategies for using your library effectively.

Key topics:

→ The range of facilities and resources
→ What you need to know as a borrower
→ Regulations and codes of conduct
→ Key library skills

Key terms
Copyright   Dewey decimal system   ebrary   Information literacy
Library of Congress system

The library is a key resource for any student. A modern university library is much more than a collection of books and journals – it co-ordinates an electronic gateway to a vast amount of online information. Accessing these resources requires information literacy skills that are essential for essay and assignment writing.

→ The range of facilities and resources

Most university libraries offer the following facilities:

● quiet study areas;
● groupwork areas where discussion is allowed;
● photocopiers and printers;

- computing terminals, and possibly a wireless network;
- online catalogue access;
- support from expert staff, both in person and via the library website.

Apart from books, most UK university libraries will also hold the following, in hard copy or with free online access:

- selected daily and weekly newspapers;
- periodicals and academic journals;
- reference materials;
- slides (e.g. for art or life sciences); and
- video and DVD resources.

Table 5.1 indicates the type of content you can expect from these resources. The precise holdings will depend on factors such as the degrees taught, any teaching specialisms, the research interests of staff and past bequests of collections. Each library is unique and, in this respect, will hold particular archive material that is not available elsewhere.

Should I buy textbook(s)?

Sometimes reading lists are lengthy and the recommended textbooks are expensive. It's worth purchasing your own copy of books that you need to refer to frequently and that relate strongly to the lecture content and coursework. In other cases, it's worth checking what the library holds, although you may encounter access problems if everyone else in the class is looking for the same thing at the same time. In this case, use the catalogue to find alternatives – there are usually other options. If you are not sure how to do this, then ask a librarian for help.

E-resources

Many current items are now available online in each of the categories listed in Table 5.1. For example, libraries take out subscriptions to e-book repositories, e-journals, e-newspapers and online dictionaries and encyclopaedias. Your institution will have its own method of giving access to these resources, probably via the library electronic desktop. A password may be required (see p. 61).

Table 5.1 **Some of the types of content that can be obtained from library resources.** These may be available as hard copy or online.

Type of resource	Examples	Indication of content
Books	Prescribed texts	Provide clear linkage with the course content
	General textbooks	Give an overview of the subject
	Supplementary texts	Discuss subject in greater depth
Reference books	Standard dictionaries	Provide spelling, pronunciation and meaning
	Bilingual dictionaries	Provide translation of words and expressions in two languages
	Subject-specific dictionaries	Define key specialist terms
	General encyclopaedias	Provide a quick overview of a new topic
	Discipline-specific encyclopaedias	Focus on in-depth coverage of specific topics
	Biographical material	Sources of information on key figures both contemporary and in the past
	Yearbooks	Provide up-to-date information on organisations
	Atlases	Provide geographical or historical information
	Directories	Provide up-to-date access to information on organisations
Newspapers	Daily or weekly newspapers	Provide coverage of contemporary issues
Periodicals and academic journals	Discipline- or subject-specific publications produced three or four times per year	Provide recent ideas, reports and comment on current research issues
Popular periodicals	For example, *Nature; New Scientist; The Economist*	Provide coverage of emerging themes within broad fields, such as their titles suggest

The main advantage of this method of accessing information is that it is available 24 hours per day from any computer connected to the Internet. In some cases, more than one person can access the e-book at any one time. Some e-book facilities, such as ebrary, offer additional facilities, such as searching, note-making facilities and linked online dictionaries for checking the meanings of words.

Electronic databases make it easier to access information from public bodies, and much of that kind of information is also now more readily available online. For example, statistical population details are available through the National Statistics website (**www.statistics.gov.uk**), while papers and publications produced by the Houses of Parliament can also be accessed electronically (**www.parliament.uk**).

Shared library resources

Many university libraries share resources with those of neighbouring institutions and all are linked to the British Library, the national library of the UK. This receives a copy of every publication produced in the UK and Ireland, and its massive collection of over 150 million items increases by 3 million items every year. Some university libraries are designated as European Documentation Centres (**http://europa.eu.int/comm/relays/edc_en.htm**). These centres hold key documents of the European Union.

→ What you need to know as a borrower

In most cases, you will not be allowed to borrow hard copies of periodicals. You may, however, be allowed to take out books in certain categories. You should find out the answers to the following questions regarding book borrowing.

- **How many books can you borrow at any one time?** This depends on your status as a borrower: staff and postgraduate students can usually borrow more books than undergraduate members.
- **What is the maximum loan period?** This will depend on the type of resource you wish to borrow. For example, some books that are heavily in demand because they are prescribed texts may be put on a short-loan system within the library. The basic idea is that readers are limited to a shorter borrowing time for these books. This period may be as short as a few hours, or perhaps a few days. Standard loans are usually for several weeks.
- **What are the fines if you keep a book after the due date?** Fines usually apply to all borrowers, whether they are staff or

students. The fine will be dictated by the status of the book that is overdue. Short-loan books have higher fines; standard loans are lower. While a few pence may not seem much on a standard loan, if you have 10 books all overdue for two weeks, you can be looking at a double-figure in pounds.

- **How can you renew the loan?** Alternatives to doing this in person include telephone renewals, and, in many cases, online facilities enable you to renew books from wherever you can access your university home page.

Electronic book tagging

To protect their valuable assets, most universities operate a system of electronic 'book tagging' to ensure that resources cannot be withdrawn without being logged out to a particular user. This means that all books need to be 'de-activated' before you can take them out of the library.

→ Regulations and codes of conduct

All libraries have these; they generally serve to protect the resources and respect the needs of other library users. You will be alerted to these rules by notices, leaflets and websites. In particular, you have important legal responsibilities under copyright law, which sets out limits on the amount of material you can photocopy (**Ch 17**).

→ Key library skills

These are the basic skills you will need to master:

- **How to use the electronic catalogue.** Most systems offer a function where you can search by author, by title, or by subject, although there may be more options on the system you will use.
- **How to find a book or periodical.** When you identify the book that you want from the catalogue, then you need to be able to find where it is shelved in the library. This means that you need to take a note of two things: the location (the book might be

shelved in another site library, for example) and the class number (not the ISBN number, which is not relevant here). The catalogue number may comprise a sequence of letters and/or numbers depending on the system used in your library. This number corresponds to the number on the spine of the book – universities generally use one of two systems (see the information box below). Books are shelved sequentially according to these numbers in stacks labelled to assist you to find what you want. If you have difficulty in locating a particular book, then library staff can help.

● **How to borrow a book or journal from another library.** Sometimes books are not available in your own library and you may wish to request a loan from another UK library. There will be a particular librarian responsible for inter-library loans who will arrange this. However, there are cost implications in this process. Usually, the cost is borne by the borrower, not the library.

Catalogue searches

smart tip

It is useful to remember that there are often several ways to spell surnames, for example Brown/Browne or Nichol/Nicol/Nicoll. To find a book by an author whose name you may only have heard mentioned in a lecture, you may have to try various options. Check with the book list in your course handbook, as this may give details, including catalogue information.

Library cataloguing systems

The system your library uses will be explained in leaflets or during the library tour. The two main possibilities are:

■ **The Dewey decimal system:** each book is given a numerical code. For example, editions of *Hamlet* by William Shakespeare are filed under 822.33.

■ **The Library of Congress system:** each book is given an alphanumeric code. For example, editions of *Hamlet* by William Shakespeare are filed under PR2807.

Additional numbers and letters may be used to define editions and variants on a subject area. Each system may be interpreted slightly differently in different libraries.

- **How to access your university library's e-resources.** This is normally done via the library's website. Some resources are open-access, but others will require a password. The *Athens* username and password scheme allows publishers to verify that your library has subscribed to an e-resource and that you have access rights. You'll normally need to log on to a university network computer to obtain an *Athens* account, but once you have received the username and password information, you can log in from any Internet-connected computer.

Of course, finding information within the library and associated online facilities is only the first step in using it for your studies. The next stage is to evaluate it and use it appropriately in your note-making and academic writing (**Ch 6** and **Ch 10**). In these contexts, citing sources of information correctly is important, to avoid plagiarism (**Ch 17** and **Ch 18**).

Practical tips for making the most of library resources

Go on a library tour. Be prepared to ask questions if you are shown things that you don't understand or that seem strange to you. University libraries are unlike public libraries in many ways and have much more to offer. This is a chance to learn about these opportunities. If tours are not available, then see if a virtual tour can be made from your university library's website.

Find out who specialises in your area within the library. This person can help you with any difficulties you encounter and could be a very useful ally.

Take advantage of reciprocal arrangements. Some university libraries have agreements with other similar libraries in the area, including national libraries. This enables you to use and sometimes, depending on the agreement, to borrow books from partner libraries.

Find and join the local public library. This may hold some texts that would be relevant to your course and will not be so heavily in demand as those in the university library.

5.1 Spend some time becoming thoroughly acquainted with the electronic library resources. Look, in particular, at any subject-specific resources that are provided on the catalogue system or via the library website. There may also be valuable pointers on your course web pages or within your online learning environment.

5.2 Explore the shelves covering your subject area. Identify this area from the library catalogue and the information on shelving aisles. 'Browsing' the books and catalogues may reveal interesting resources you might not find by other searching methods.

5.3 Find out about alternative library facilities. In some cases, there may be satellite libraries on different campuses or in different buildings. Some of these may be departmental libraries, containing specialist resources. These can contain duplicate holdings of books in the main library. Importantly, you may find they represent convenient or preferable study areas. Even if they do not cover your subject area, you may find that their atmosphere is more suited to your mood, learning style or personality.

6 | Note-making from texts

How to create effective notes for later reference

Keeping a record of the content of your reading and its relevance to your set task is essential. There is simply too much information to remember and retain. This chapter outlines practical ways in which you can keep a record of what you read in appropriate note form so that it is meaningful to you when writing an assignment.

Key topics:
→ Why are you taking notes?
→ What do you need to record?
→ How are you going to lay out your notes?

Key terms
Annotate   Citation   Citing   Landscape orientation   Mnemonic
Portrait orientation

Most courses provide a reading list of recommended resources. Depending on your subject, these include textbooks, journal articles and web-based materials. Sometimes you will be given specific references; at other times you will have to find the relevant material in the text for yourself. The techniques described in **Ch 4** will help you identify the most relevant parts of the text quickly and provide basic information for your note-making.

You will develop note-making skills as you progress in your studies. It takes time and experimentation to achieve a method that suits you. This will need to fit with your learning style, the time that you can allocate to the task and be appropriate for the material and the subject area you are tackling. This chapter suggests a range of methods you can choose to help you abstract and write down the key points from your sources.

→ Why are you taking notes?

Depending on your task, you may need to assimilate and manipulate information from a range of information sources, such as textbooks, journal articles, reviews or websites. Some sources will simply be 'dip in and out', while some will require intensive reading. You need to decide what your purpose is in making the notes. For example, it may be to:

- frame an overview of the subject;
- record a sequence or process;
- enable you to analyse a problem;
- extract the logic of an argument;
- compare different viewpoints;
- borrow quotes (with suitable citation - see **Ch 18**); or
- add your own commentary on the text, perhaps by linking key points with what has been discussed in a lecture or tutorial.

This will influence the style, detail and depth of your notes.

---

smart tip

Essentials of note-making

It will save time if you develop good practice in making your notes.

- On all notes record the full details of source, that is:
  - author surname and initials
  - title in full with chapter and pages
  - date of publication
  - publisher and place of publication.

You will need these details to enable you to cite the source of information if you decide to use any of this information in your own writing (**Ch 18**).

- It's a good idea to add the date(s) you made the notes.
- Your notes should be meaningful in six days', weeks' or months' time. Personalise them by using:
  - underlining
  - highlighting
  - colour coding
  - numbered lists
  - bullet points
  - mnemonics
  - distinctive layout
  - boxes for important points.

→ What do you need to record?

One of the pitfalls of making notes is that people often start off with a blank sheet, pen in hand, and then begin to note 'important' points as they read. Within a short time, they are rewriting the book. To avoid this, the trick is to:

- identify your purpose in relation to the assignment task;
- scan the section to be read;
- establish the writer's purpose, for example:
  - a narrative of events or process
  - a statement of facts
  - an explanation of reasoning or presentation of a logical argument
  - an analysis of an issue, problem or situation
  - a critique of an argument;
- work out their 'take' on the subject, and how this relates to your purpose;
- decide on the most appropriate note-making style and layout for the task;
- Ensure you paraphrase in your own words rather than transcribe; but if you do transcribe, use quote marks and note reference details.

→ How are you going to lay out your notes?

There are several strategies that you might consider using. Figures 6.1–6.7 illustrate some examples. Not all will be relevant to your subject, but some will. Some techniques may not seem directly suitable, but, with a little adaptation, they may work for you. Table 6.8 compares the advantages and disadvantages of each method.

---

smart tip

Note-making formats

Sometimes notes may be better suited to being laid out on paper in the landscape rather than the portrait position. This clearly suits methods such as concept maps (Figure 6.5). Similarly, you can take advantage of the landscape format when making matrix (grid) notes (Figure 6.6) by creating columns across the page.

Topic: DEPOPULATION OF THE COUNTRYSIDE   Source: Ormiston, J., 2002. Rural Idylls.
                                           Glasgow: Country Press.

Problem: Population falling in rural areas
                  Traditional communities disintegrate
                  Incomer settlement – dormitory villages

Reasons: Mechanisation of farming
                  Creation of farming combines
                  Bigger farms, fewer employed
                  Decline of traditional farming & related activities

Effects: Families dispersed – fewer children
                  Closure of shops, post offices, schools, surgeries
                  Transport links less viable

Solutions: Housing subsidies to encourage families to remain
                  Diversify economic activity, e.g. tourism/action holidays
                  Stimulate rural economy – farm shops, farmers' markets
                  Diversify from traditional crops – seek new markets

Figure 6.1 Example of keyword notes.

Topic: OBESITY IN CHILDREN   Source: Skinner, J., 2001. Diet and Obesity.
                                        Edinburgh: Castle Publishing.

1. Lifestyle
   1.1 Television, computer-games generation
   1.2 Unsupervised leisure time – sedentary
2. Diet
   2.1 Constant 'grazing' – junk food
   2.2 Additives/processed foods
   2.3 Lack of adequate fresh food, including fruit + vegetables
3. Exercise
   3.1 Sport by spectating rather than participating
   3.2 Decline in team sports in schools
   3.3 Children over-protected from 'free play' outdoors
4. Family
   4.1 Parents overeat; children likewise
   4.2 Instant food
   4.3 Food as an incentive + reward
5. Schools
   5.1 School meals spurned in favour of snack bar/chip shop
   5.2 Healthy–eating programmes as part of curriculum
6. Health service
   6.1 Less emphasis on prevention
   6.2 Limited health education of parents and children

(a)

Figure 6.2 Examples of linear notes. These are samples drawn from three diverse disciplines where topics lend themselves to hierarchical approaches.

Figure 6.2 continued

Topic:
GENERAL FEATURES OF ORGANIC MATERIALS

Source: Barker, J., 2001. Chemistry for University. Manchester: Midland Publishing.

1. Solid state – molec. crystal – powder, poly. Thin films
2. Unique physical properties – exploit for high-tech applications
3. Advantages
    3.1 Versatile properties – reg. by organic chemistry
    3.2 Readily accessible – via organic synthesis
    3.3 Low cost – cheap raw materials
    3.4 Tractable – fusable, soluble: easy to fab.
4. Disadvantage
    4.1 Relatively fragile
5. Important types
    5.1 Conducting CT salts
    5.2 Conducting poly

(b)

Topic: **OPERATIONAL AMPLIFIERS**

Source: Scott, D.I., 1977. Operational Amplifiers. Coventry: Circuit Publishers.

1. Usually an integrated circuit; can be discrete
2. Uses all technologies: bipolar; FET; MOS; BI-FET
3. Effectively a highly stable differential amplifier
4. Advantages
    4.1 High voltage gain – typ. 100,000
    4.2 High input impedance – typ. $1M\Omega$ – can be much higher, FET, MOS
    4.3 Low output impedance – typ. 600Ω
    4.4 Low drift, BI-FET best
    4.5 Wide supply voltage range
5. Disadvantages
    5.1 Relatively narrow bandwidth – GBP typ. 1MHz (but operates to DC)
    5.2 Very unstable in discrete versions – requires matched transistors
6. Common types
    6.1 741 – most common
    6.2 LM 380 – common AF AMP
    6.3 TDA 2030 – common power amp. – 20W into 4Ω

(c)

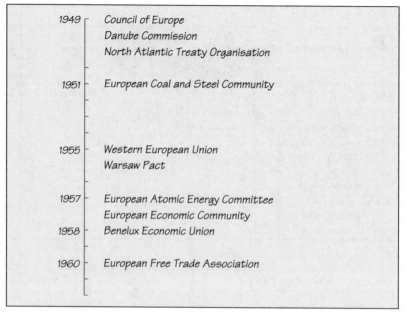

Figure 6.3 Example of time-line notes. This design is good for showing a sequence of events, in this case, the development of European organisations.

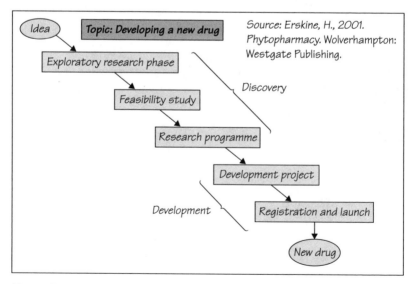

Figure 6.4 Example of flow-chart notes. These are particularly useful for describing complex processes in visual form.

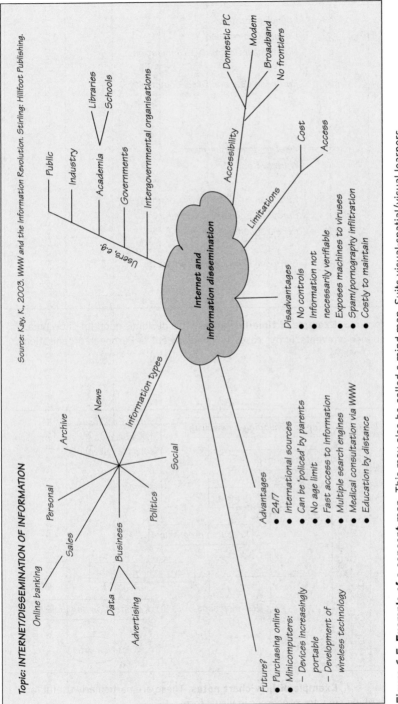

Topic: INTERNET/DISSEMINATION OF INFORMATION

Source: Kay, K., 2003. WWW and the Information Revolution. Stirling: Hillfoot Publishing.

Internet and information dissemination

Users, e.g.
- Public
- Industry
- Academia
  - Libraries
  - Schools
- Governments
- Intergovernmental organisations

Accessibility
- Domestic PC
- Modem
- Broadband
- No frontiers

Limitations
- Cost
- Access

Disadvantages
- No controls
- Information not necessarily verifiable
- Exposes machines to viruses
- Spam/pornography infiltration
- Costly to maintain

Information types
- Online banking
- Sales
- Personal
- Data
- Business
  - Advertising
- Archive
- News
- Social
- Politics

Advantages
- 24/7
- International sources
- Can be 'policed' by parents
- No age limit
- Fast access to information
- Multiple search engines
- Medical consultation via WWW
- Education by distance

Future?
- Purchasing online
- Minicomputers:
  - Devices increasingly portable
  - Development of wireless technology

Figure 6.5 Example of a concept map. This may also be called a mind map. Suits visual-spatial/visual learners.

Topic: TRAFFIC CONGESTION

Source: Walker, I.M.A., 2005. Urban Myths and Motorists. London: Green Press.

Solutions	Council view	Police view	Local business view	Local community view
Pedestrianisation	+ Low maintenance − Initial outlay	+ Easier to police + Less car crime + CCTV surveillance easier	+ Safer shopping and business activity − Discourages motorist customers	+ Safer shopping + Less polluted town/city environment
Park and ride schemes	+ Implements transport policy − Capital investment to initiate − Car park maintenance	+ Reduce inner-city/town traffic jams + Reduce motor accidents − Potential car park crime	− Loss of custom − Lack of convenience − Sends customers elsewhere	+ Less polluted town/city environment − Costly
Increase parking charges	+ Revenue from fines − Costly to set up	− Hostility to enforcers	− Loss of custom − Delivery unloading problematic	− Residents penalised by paying for on-street parking
Restrict car journeys, e.g. odd/even registrations on alternate days	+ Easy to administer	+ Easy to police	− Seek exemption for business vehicles	+ Encourage car-sharing for daily journeys − Inconvenience
Levy congestion charge for urban journeys	+ Revenue raised − Cost of implementing tracking system	− Traffic jams on alternative routes	− Cost of loss of custom	− Inhibit work/leisure activities − Cost

Figure 6.6 Example of matrix notes. This particular analysis lays out positive (+) and negative (−) viewpoints on an issue from a range of different perspectives.

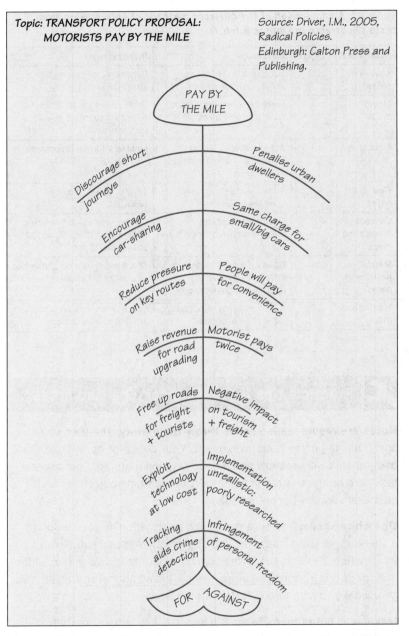

Topic: TRANSPORT POLICY PROPOSAL: MOTORISTS PAY BY THE MILE

Source: Driver, I.M., 2005, Radical Policies. Edinburgh: Calton Press and Publishing.

PAY BY THE MILE

Discourage short journeys

Penalise urban dwellers

Encourage car-sharing

Same charge for small/big cars

Reduce pressure on key routes

People will pay for convenience

Raise revenue for road upgrading

Motorist pays twice

Free up roads for freight + tourists

Negative impact on tourism + freight

Exploit technology at low cost

Implementation unrealistic: poorly researched

Tracking aids crime detection

Infringement of personal freedom

FOR   AGAINST

Figure 6.7 Example of a herringbone map. This design is good for showing, as in this case, two sides to an argument. May be particularly appealing to visual learners.

Table 6.1 A comparison of the different methods of note-making from texts (illustrated in Figures 6.1–6.7)

Note type	Figure	Advantage	Disadvantage
Keyword notes	6.1	Good as a layout for easy access to information	Dependent on systematic structure in text
Linear notes	6.2	Numbered sequence – good for classifying ideas	Restrictive format, difficult to backtrack to insert new information
Time lines	6.3	Act as memory aid for a sequence of events; stages in a process	Limited information possible
Flow-chart notes	6.4	Allow clear path through complex options	Take up space; may be unwieldy
Concept maps/mind maps	6.5	Good for recording information on a single page	Can become messy; can be difficult to follow; not suited to all learning styles
Matrix notes/grid notes	6.6	Good layout for recording different viewpoints, approaches, applications	Space limitations on content or amount of information
Herringbone maps	6.7	Good for laying out opposing sides of an argument	Space limitations on content or amount of information

 Practical tips for making personalised notes

Notes are resources, so never throw them away. The time you spend making notes is an investment. Your notes for essays and assignments will probably make good revision material. Coursework tasks are often revisited in exams – check learning objectives and past exam papers to confirm this.

Use white space. Don't cram as much information as you can on to a sheet; leave white space around lists or other important items of information. By using the 'visual' part of your brain, you will recall the imprint of this information more easily. This additional space can also be used if you wish to add further detail later.

Make your notes memorable. It's important to make sure that your notes are visually striking. However, spending lots of time making them look pretty will not necessarily pay dividends. Again, try to achieve a balance – visually memorable enough to trigger your recall but not so elaborate that they become a meaningless work of art without substance.

Develop your own 'shorthand'. Some subjects have their own abbreviations, for example MI (myocardial infarction) or WTO (World Trade Organisation) and, of course, there are standard abbreviations – e.g., i.e., etc. However, you will also develop your own abbreviations and symbols drawn from your own experience, for example, maths symbols, text messaging or words from other languages. As long as these are memorable and meaningful to you, then they can be useful tools in making and taking notes.

Save time using a photocopy. Sometimes you may find that the extent of notes you require is minimal, or that a particular book or other resource is in high demand and has been placed on short loan in the library. It may be convenient to photocopy the relevant pages, which can then be highlighted and annotated. Remember that there are photocopying restrictions imposed on readers due to copyright law (**Ch 17**) – details will be posted prominently in your library.

Take care when using material straight from the text. It is important that, if you decide to use an excerpt from a text as a direct quotation, you record the page number on which that particular piece of text appeared in the book or article you are citing. You should then insert the author, date of publication and page number alongside the quotation. More information on citing sources is given in **Ch 18** and **Ch 17**.

GO **And now . . .**

6.1 Find out about abbreviations. Find a general dictionary that gives a comprehensive list of abbreviations and identify ones that you might use; find a subject-specific dictionary and identify whether it provides lists of specialist abbreviations. This will mean that you'll know where to look if you come across an abbreviation that is unfamiliar to you.

6.2 Compare notes with a friend. Everyone has a different method of note-making that they have personalised to suit their own style. Compare your note-making style with that of a fellow student – preferably on the same piece of text. Discuss what you have recorded and why – this may bring out some differences in reasoning, understanding and logic.

▶

6.3 Try something different. You may feel that you already have a fairly reasonable note-making strategy in place, but as time goes on you may find that it is not quite as suitable for the type of reading you are now required to do. If this turns out to be the case, then try out some of the alternative styles demonstrated in this chapter to see if these are better suited to your study tasks.

7 | Thinking critically

How to develop a logical approach to analysis, synthesis and evaluation

The ability to think critically is probably the most transferable of the skills you will develop at university – and one that it is vital to develop if you wish to gain excellent marks in essays and assignments. This chapter introduces concepts, methods and fallacies to watch out for when trying to improve your analytical capabilities.

Key topics:
- → Thinking about thinking
- → Using method to prompt and organise your thoughts
- → Recognising fallacies and biased presentations

Key terms
Bias   Critical thinking   Fallacy   Propaganda   Value judgement

Many specialists believe that critical thinking is a skill that you can develop through practice – and this assumption lies behind much university teaching. Your experience of the educational system probably tells you that your marks depend increasingly on the analysis of facts and the ability to arrive at an opinion and support it with relevant information, rather than the simple recall of fact. If you understand the underlying processes a little better, this should help you meet your tutors' expectations. Also, adopting a methodical approach can be useful when you are unsure how to tackle a new task.

> **Definition: critical**
>
> People often interpret the words 'critical' and 'criticism' to mean being negative about an issue. For university work, the alternative meaning of 'making a careful judgement after balanced consideration of all aspects of a topic' is the one you should adopt.

Benjamin Bloom, a noted educational psychologist, and his colleagues, identified six different steps involved in learning and thinking within education:

- knowledge
- comprehension
- application
- analysis
- synthesis
- evaluation.

Bloom *et al.* (1956) showed that students naturally progressed through this scale of thought-processing during their studies (Table 7.1). Looking at this table, you may recognise that your school work mainly focussed on knowledge, comprehension and application, while your university tutors tend to expect more in terms of analysis, synthesis and evaluation. These expectations are sometimes closely linked to

Table 7.1 **Bloom *et al.*'s classification of thinking processes (Bloom's taxonomy)**

Thinking processes (in ascending order of difficulty)	Typical question instructions
Knowledge. If you know a fact, you have it at your disposal and can *recall* or *recognise* it. This does not mean you necessarily understand it at a higher level.	• Define • Describe • Identify
Comprehension. To comprehend a fact means that you *understand* what it means.	• Contrast • Discuss • Interpret
Application. To apply a fact means that you can *put it to use.*	• Demonstrate • Calculate • Illustrate
Analysis. To analyse information means that you are able to *break it down into parts* and show how these components *fit together.*	• Analyse • Explain • Compare
Synthesis. To synthesise, you need to be able to *extract relevant facts* from a body of knowledge and use these to *address an issue in a novel way* or *create something new.*	• Compose • Create • Integrate
Evaluation. If you evaluate information, you *arrive at a judgement* based on its importance relative to the topic being addressed.	• Recommend • Support • Draw a conclusion

the instruction words used in assessments, and Table 7.1 provides a few examples. However, take care when interpreting these, as processes and tasks may mean different things in different subjects. For example, while 'description' might imply a lower-level activity in the sciences, it might involve high-level skills in subjects like architecture.

Some disciplines value creativity as a thinking process, for example, art and design, architecture, drama or English composition. In such cases, this word might take the place of synthesis in Table 7.1. Some people also propose that in certain cases creativity should be placed higher than evaluation in the table.

When you analyse the instructions used in writing assignments, you should take into account what type of thinking process the examiner has asked you to carry out, and try your best to reach the required level. To help you understand what might be required, Table 7.2 gives examples of thought processes you might experience in a range of areas of study.

Contents for thinking critically

Examples of university assignments involving high-level thinking skills include:

■ essay-writing in the arts and social sciences
■ reports on problem-based learning in medicine and nursing
■ case-based scenarios in law
■ reports on project-based practical work in the sciences

→ Using method to prompt and organise your thoughts

Suppose you recognise that critical thinking is required to address a particular task. This could be an essay question set by one of your tutors, an issue arising from problem-based learning, or even a domestic matter such as what type of car to buy or where best to rent a flat. The pointers below help you to arrive at a logical answer. You should regard this as a menu rather than a recipe – think about the different stages and how they might be useful for the specific task under consideration and your own style of work. Adopt or reject them as you see fit, or, according to your needs, chop and change their order.

Table 7.2 Examples of thinking processes within representative university subjects (Bloom et al., 1956)

Thinking processes (in ascending order of difficulty)	Law	Examples — Arts subjects, e.g. History or Politics	Numerical subjects
Knowledge	You might know the name and date of a case, statute or treaty without understanding its relevance	You might know that a river was an important geographical and political boundary in international relations, without being able to identify why	You might be able to write down a particular mathematical equation, without understanding what the symbols mean or where it might be applied
Comprehension	You would understand the principle of law contained in the legislation or case law, and its wider context	You would understand that the river forms a natural barrier, which can be easily identified and defended	You would understand what the symbols in an equation mean and how and when to apply it
Application	You would be able to identify situations to which the principle of law would apply	You might use this knowledge to explain the terms of a peace treaty	You would be able to use the equation to obtain a result, given background information
Analysis	You could relate the facts of a particular scenario to the principle to uncover the extent of its application, using appropriate authority	You could explain the river as a boundary being of importance to the territorial gains/losses for signatories to the peace treaty	You could explain the theoretical process involved in deriving the equation
Synthesis	By a process of reasoning and analogy, you could predict how the law might be applied under given circumstances	You could identify this fact and relate it to the recurrence of this issue in later treaties or factors governing further hostilities and subsequent implications	You would be able to take one equation, link it with another and arrive at a new mathematical relationship or conclusion
Evaluation	You might be able to advise a client based on your own judgement, after weighing up and evaluating all available options	You would be able to discuss whether the use of this boundary was an obstacle to resolving the terms of the treaty to the satisfaction of all parties	You would be able to discuss the limitations of an equation based on its derivation and the underlying assumptions behind this

- **Making sure you fully grasp the nature of the task.** If a specific question has been given as part of the exercise, then analyse its phrasing carefully to make sure you understand all possible meanings. If you have been given a general topic, rather than a detailed question or instruction, then write down a brief description of the aspects you wish to address – this will help you to clarify the terminology and concepts involved.

- **Organise your approach to the task.** You might start with a 'brainstorm' to identify potential solutions or viewpoints. This can be a solo or group activity and typically might consist of three phases:
  - **Open thinking.** Consider the issue or question from all possible angles or positions and write down everything you come up with. Don't worry at this stage about the relevance or importance of your ideas. You may wish to use a 'spider diagram' or 'mind map' to lay out your thoughts (Figure 6.5).
  - **Organisation.** Next, you should try to arrange your ideas into categories or sub-headings, or group them as supporting or opposing a viewpoint. A new diagram, table or grid may be useful to make things clear.
  - **Analysis.** Now you need to decide about the relevance of the grouped points to the original problem. Reject trivial or irrelevant ideas and rank or prioritise those that seem relevant.

- **Get background information and check your comprehension of the facts.** It's quite likely that you will need to gather relevant information and ideas – to support your thoughts, provide examples or suggest a range of interpretations or approaches. You also need to ensure you fully understand the information you have gathered. This could be as simple as using dictionaries and technical works to find out the precise meaning of key words; it might involve discussing your ideas with your peers or a tutor; or you could read a range of texts to see how others interpret your topic.

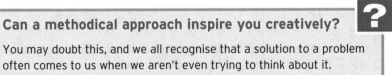

Can a methodical approach inspire you creatively?

You may doubt this, and we all recognise that a solution to a problem often comes to us when we aren't even trying to think about it. However, technique can sometimes help you clarify the issues, organise the evidence and arrive at a balanced answer. This should help inspiration to follow.

- **Check relevance.** Now consider the information you have gathered, your thoughts and how these might apply to your question. You may need to re-analyse the question. You will then need to marshal the evidence you have collected – for example: for or against a proposition; supporting or opposing an argument or theory. You may find it useful to prepare a table or grid to organise the information (Figure 6.6) – this will also help you balance your thoughts. Be ruthless in rejecting irrelevant or inconsequential material.

- **Think through your argument, and how you can support it.** Having considered relevant information and positions, you should arrive at a personal viewpoint, and then construct your discussion or conclusion around this. When writing about your topic, you must take care to avoid value judgements or other kinds of expression of opinion that are not supported by evidence or sources. This is one reason why frequent citation and referencing is demanded in academic work.

- **Get cracking on your answer.** Once you have decided on what you want to say, writing it up should be much easier.

→ Recognising fallacies and biased presentations

As you consider arguments and discussions on academic subjects, you will notice that various linguistic devices are used to promote particular points of view. Identifying these is a valuable aspect of critical thinking, allowing you to detach yourself from the argument itself and think about the way in which it is being conducted.

Definitions

- **Fallacy:** a fault in logic or thinking that means that an argument is incorrect.
- **Bias:** information that emphasises just one viewpoint or position.
- **Propaganda:** false or incomplete information that supports a (usually) extreme political or moral view.

There are many different types of logical fallacies, and Table 7.3 lists only a few common examples. Once tuned in to this way of thinking, you should observe that faulty logic and debating tricks are frequently used in areas such as advertising and politics. Analysing the methods being used can be a useful way of practising your critical-thinking skills.

One way of avoiding bias in your own written work is consciously to try to balance your discussion. Avoid 'absolutes' – be careful with words that imply that there are no exceptions, for example, *always, never, all* and *every*. These words can only be used if you are absolutely sure of facts that imply 100 per cent certainty.

Practical tips for thinking critically

Focus on the task in hand. It is very easy to become distracted when reading around a subject, or when discussing problems with others. Take care not to waste too much time on preliminaries and start relevant action as quickly as possible.

Write down your thoughts. The act of writing your thoughts is important as this forces you to clarify them. Also, since ideas are often fleeting, it makes sense to ensure you have a permanent record. Reviewing what you have written makes you more critical and can lead you on to new ideas.

Table 7.3 **Common examples of logical fallacies, bias and propaganda techniques found in arguments.** There are many different types of fallacious arguments (at least 70) and this is an important area of study in philosophical logic.

Type of fallacy or propaganda	Description	Example	How to counteract this approach
Ad hominem (Latin for 'to the man')	An attack is made on the character of the person putting forward an argument, rather than on the argument itself; this is particularly common in the media and politics	The President's moral behaviour is suspect, so his financial policies must also be dubious	Suggest that the person's character or circumstances are irrelevant
Ad populum (Latin for 'to the people')	The argument is supported on the basis that it is a popular viewpoint; of course, this does not make it correct in itself	The majority of people support corporal punishment for vandals, so we should introduce boot camps	Watch out for bandwagons and peer-pressure effects and ignore them when considering rights and wrongs
Anecdotal evidence	Use of unrepresentative exceptions to contradict an argument based on statistical evidence	My gran was a heavy smoker and she lived to be 95, so smoking won't harm me	Consider the overall weight of evidence rather than isolated examples
Appeal to authority	An argument is supported on the basis that an expert or authority agrees with the conclusion; used in advertisements, where celebrity endorsement and testimonials are frequent	My professor, whom I admire greatly, believes in Smith's theory, so it must be right	Point out that the experts do disagree and explain how and why; focus on the key qualities of the item or argument

Appeal to ignorance	Because there's no evidence for (or against) a case, it means the case must be false (or true)	You haven't an alibi, therefore you must be guilty	Point out that a conclusion either way may not be possible in the absence of evidence
Biased evidence	Selection of examples or evidence for or against a case. A writer who quotes those who support their view, but not those against	My advisers tell me that global warming isn't going to happen.	Read around the subject, including those with a different view, and try to arrive at a balanced opinion.
Euphemisms and jargon	Use of phrasing to hide the true position or exaggerate an opponent's – stating things in mild or emotive language for effect; use of technical words to sound authoritative	My job as vertical transportation operative means I am used to being in a responsible position	Watch for (unnecessary) adjectives, noun strings or adverbs that may affect the way you consider the evidence
Repetition	Saying the same thing over and over again until people believe it. Common in politics, war propaganda and advertising	'Beanz means Heinz'	Look out for repeated catchphrases and lack of substantive argument
Straw man/false dichotomy	A position is misrepresented in order to create a diversionary debating point that is easily accepted or rejected, when in fact the core issue has not been addressed	Asylum seekers all want to milk the benefits system, so we should turn them all away	Point out the fallacy and focus on the core issue

Try to be analytical, not descriptive. By looking at Table 7.1, you will appreciate why analysis is regarded as a higher-level skill than description. Many students lose marks because they simply quote facts or statements, without explaining their importance and context, that is, without showing their understanding of what the quote means or implies.

When quoting evidence, use appropriate citations. This is important as it shows you have read relevant source material and helps you avoid plagiarism (**Ch 17**). The conventions for citation vary among subjects, so consult course handbooks or other information and make sure you follow the instructions carefully, or you may lose marks (**Ch 18**).

Draw on the ideas and opinions of your peers and tutors. Discussions with others can be very fruitful, revealing a range of interpretations that you might not have thought about yourself. You may find it useful to bounce ideas off others. Tutors can provide useful guidance once you have done some reading, and are usually pleased to be asked for help.

Keep an open mind. Although you may start with preconceived ideas about a topic, you should try to be receptive to the ideas of others. You may find that your initial thoughts become altered by what you are reading and discussing. If there is not enough evidence to support *any* conclusion, be prepared to suspend judgement.

Look beneath the surface. Decide whether sources are dealing with facts or opinions; examine any assumptions made, including your own; think about the motivation of writers. Rather than restating and describing your sources, focus on what they *mean* by what they write.

Avoid common pitfalls of shallow thinking. Try not to:

- rush to conclusions;
- generalise;
- oversimplify;
- personalise;
- use fallacious arguments;
- think in terms of stereotypes;
- make value judgements.

Keep asking yourself questions. A good way to think more deeply is to ask questions, even after you feel a matter is resolved or you understand it well. All critical thinking is the result of asking questions.

Balance your arguments. If asked to arrive at a position on a subject, you should try to do this in an even-handed way, by considering all possible viewpoints and by presenting your conclusion with supporting evidence.

 And now . . .

7.1 Practise seeing both sides of an argument. Choose a topic, perhaps one on which you have strong views (for example, a political matter, such as state support for private schooling; or an ethical one, such as the need for vivisection or abortion). Write down the supporting arguments for both sides of the issue, focusing on your least-favoured option. This will help you see both sides of a debate as a matter of course.

7.2 Analyse the instruction words in past exam papers. Note which types of instruction words are commonly used. First check that you understand what is expected in relation to each word, then, taking into account the subject and the way in which it has been taught, what level of thinking you are expected to demonstrate in your exam answers. If you are in doubt, ask a subject tutor to explain.

7.3 Look into the murky world of fallacies and biased arguments. There are some very good websites that provide lists of different types of these with examples. Investigate these by using 'fallacy' or 'logical fallacies' in a search engine. Not only are the results quite entertaining at times, but you will find the knowledge obtained improves your analytical and debating skills.

Writing the first draft

8   Academic writing formats

How to organise your writing within a standard framework

Regardless of the type of writing assignment you have to complete, the structure will follow a basic format. This chapter describes this design and explores some features that need to be included as you map your outline plan on to this structure.

Key topics:

→ Standard format
→ Taking word limits into account

Key terms
Citation   Exemplify

This chapter describes the essential format of any piece of academic writing, namely, introduction-main body-conclusion. It is on this basic framework that different types of academic assignment are constructed, and these are examined in detail in **Ch 9**.

→ Standard format

The basic structure follows the convention of moving from the general (the introduction) through to the specific (the main body) and back to the general (the conclusion).

Introduction

Generally, this should consist of three components:

● a brief explanation of the context of the topic;

● an outline of the topic as you understand it;

● an explanation of how you plan to address the topic in this particular text - in effect, a statement of intent.

The importance of the introduction

This is the first contact that your reader makes with you as the author of the text. This means that it has to be well organised and clear. However, to achieve this it is important to see the introductory section as 'work in progress' because, until you complete the entire text, you cannot really introduce the whole work accurately. Indeed, some people prefer to start writing the main body, move on to the conclusion, and then write the introduction.

This introductory section can be quite long as it may take several sentences to lay out these three dimensions. It's important to do this with some thought because this indicates to your reader where you expect to take them in the main body of text. The introduction also lays down the parameters that you have set yourself for this piece of text. For example, your topic may be multifaceted and the word limit imposed on the total piece of text will not allow you to give a comprehensive coverage of all aspects. It is better to acknowledge the extensive nature of the topic and note that you are going to limit your discussion to only some of these aspects – usually those you consider to be most important. You need to explain the reasons for this decision at this stage.

Main body

This section lays out your work based on the approach you decide to adopt in organising the content (**Ch 9**). You will have explained the approach in the introduction and this will mean that you should have mapped out your route for explaining your points.

Sub-headings

In some disciplines, and especially in report writing, sub-headings are acceptable. In others they are not. However, it's helpful to maintain the focus of your writing if you use sub-headings in your draft. This helps to prevent you digressing into unrelated areas or presenting an apparently rambling paper. If you then 'translate' your sub-heading into a topic sentence (**Ch 11**), this will provide a link with the previous paragraph or an introduction to the next theme.

In this section, you may need to generalise, describe, define or exemplify as part of your analysis. Here it's important to try to keep this part of the writing as concise, yet as clear, as possible. The construction of your paragraphs will be dictated by what you are trying to do at any particular point. Different types of paragraph structures are outlined in Table 11.3.

Conclusion

This summarises the whole piece of work. You should review the entire text in three elements:

- a restatement of the question or task and what you feel are the important features of the topic;
- a summary of the specific evidence that you have presented in support of your views;
- a statement of your overall viewpoint on the topic.

What mainly distinguishes the conclusion from the introduction is language. In the introduction, your explanation should be given clearly, avoiding jargon or technical words as far as possible. In the conclusion, you will be writing about the detail of the content and, therefore, the terminology you use is more likely to contain technical or more sophisticated language because you will have introduced this in the main body. You should avoid introducing new ideas in the conclusion that have not already been discussed in the earlier part of the writing.

---

smart tip

Mini-conclusions

As you become immersed in the writing process you will become very familiar with the material and conclusions you have drawn along the way. By the time you come to write the conclusion to the whole work this in-depth awareness may become diluted. To avoid this, it is a good idea, at the end of each section you write, to note down what main ideas you had considered and what your view is about these. If you note these mini-conclusions down on a separate piece of paper or a word-processed file, then this will provide the substance for your final conclusion.

→ Taking word limits into account

Word limits are imposed, not to relieve tutors of marking, but to train you to be concise in your writing and to analyse the topic carefully to decide what to keep in and what to leave out.

It's important to note that falling short of the word limit is just as bad as overrunning the maximum. Some students keep a running total of words they have used and as soon as they reach the minimum word limit, they stop abruptly. This is not a good approach because it is more likely to leave a ragged and poorly considered piece of text that comes to an unexpected halt rather than one that is well planned, relevant and concisely written.

It's usually better to plan and write your first draft keeping only a casual eye on word count at this stage. When you come to editing that draft you can prune and reshape your writing so that it becomes a tighter piece of prose that falls within the maximum–minimum word limits imposed by the regulations.

Counting words

Most word processors include a word-count feature. Microsoft Word has, in addition, a useful 'floating' toolbar that allows you to check running totals as you write or edit. You can access both features in this program from 'Tools > Word Count (> Show Toolbar)'.

Practical tips for organising your writing within a standard framework

Keep the right proportions in your response. Make sure that the three elements within your writing framework are well balanced in extent. The main body should be the most substantial piece of the writing, whereas the introduction and conclusion should occupy much less space. A common problem for many students is that they devote too much time to outlining the context in the introduction and leave themselves with too little time and space to get to the core of the essay.

Pay adequate attention to the conclusion. By the time that you come to write the conclusion, this is often done at some speed because there may be other demands on your time, or the initial interest in the subject has palled, or you may simply be tired. Thus, conclusions often don't get the attention they deserve. Do reserve some time to give your conclusion a critical appraisal, and even consider writing this section before finishing the perhaps more 'mechanical' earlier parts. Alternatively, as suggested above, you could 'write it as you go' by keeping detailed notes of key points separately as mini-conclusions, which you can use to frame your conclusion once you have written the main body.

Review the introduction. Once you have completed your draft, go back to the introduction and make sure that you have actually done what you set out to do when defining the parameters of your work and in your statement of intent. The act of writing your text may have stimulated new thoughts and your initial intentions and perceptions may have altered in the process of writing.

Think about appendices. Sometimes the length of your text may be seriously beyond the word limit. This means that some drastic 'surgery' is required. One strategy might be to remove some parts of the text and, while remaining within the word limit, reduce the information contained to bullet-point lists. The detail can then be placed in an appendix or appendices (plural of appendix), making appropriate cross-references in the main text. Clearly, this is a strategy that has to be used sparingly, but it can be useful in some situations, if allowed.

Think about citations. In many disciplines you will be expected to include reference to recognised authorities within the field you are studying – this helps to validate the ideas and concepts you are discussing. In law, this could be cases; in the arts and humanities, it could be work by a renowned academic. This does not mean that you need to quote substantial pieces of text; you can summarise the idea in your own words and then follow the rules about citation that are given in **Ch 18**. All this needs to be taken into consideration in planning and drafting your writing.

8.1 Compare textual patterns. Go back to a basic textbook and identify the proportion of space allocated to introducing the entire book or a specific chapter, and how much is reserved for the conclusion. This should be instructive in framing your own writing.

8.2 Track the pattern of your writing. Go back to an existing piece of your own writing and try to identify whether you have the basic elements and sub-elements of the standard writing format in place. Are the introduction, main body and conclusion identifiable? Does the introduction contain the elements of context, specific focus and statement of intent? For the conclusion, is your position laid out clearly and with supporting rationale? If any of the answers are negative, try to work out how you could improve things.

8.3 Practise converting sub-headings into topic sentences. Take a piece of your own writing or a section from a textbook where sub-headings have been used. Try to create a topic sentence that could replace that sub-heading. Decide which is more effective – the topic sentence or the original sub-heading. Consider why this is the case. Again, this should be instructive in shaping the style you adopt in your own writing.

Planning writing assignments

How to organise your response to the task

Once you have assembled the information for your assignment, you will be able to think about how you are going to respond to the set writing task. This chapter outlines some of the different options to consider when structuring the content of your response into an outline plan.

Key topics:

→ Identifying the key themes in your text
→ Adopting a structural approach
→ Expanding your outline

Key terms
Brainstorm   Chronological   Hierarchical

The basic framework of an essay was described in **Ch 8**. The next step is to think about the particular assignment that you have to tackle and how you might organise your response to the task. This chapter outlines the key steps in the process of planning a writing assignment.

People and their thought processes are different and so individual approaches to planning an outline response to an assignment will vary. For some people, this can be a highly detailed process; for others, it may be a minimal exercise. Too much detail in a plan can be restricting, while too little can fail to provide enough direction. Therefore, a reasonably detailed plan should give some guidance while leaving you the flexibility to alter the finer elements as you write.

→ Identifying the key themes in your text

Planning your writing means that you need to return to your 'first thoughts' brainstorm (**Ch 3**), which should have been developed further as you have added key points from your reading and thinking.

Consider whether any themes or recurrent issues are evident. It might be useful to 'colour code' all the items that are related, using a different colour highlighter for each category or theme. Then, you need to reconsider the instruction of the set task to help you construct your plan, that is, on the basis of description, analysis or argument (**Ch 3**).

Lower- or higher-order thinking?

While, for some subjects, description would be a lower-order writing activity, for others this would be considered to be a higher-order skill (see Table 7.1). Often written assignments require some initial description of context or process to outline the background to the topic. This is then followed by in-depth consideration of the topic, using more analytical or critical approaches.

→ Adopting a structural approach

Brainstorming and analysing the instruction should give you some indication of how you can construct the content of your paper as a logical discussion by considering how it might fit into one of several classic structural models or approaches (Table 9.1).

By adopting one of these models, it should be possible to map out the content of your answer in a way that provides a logical and coherent response to the task you have been set. Note that sometimes it may

Table 9.1 **The seven most common structural approaches for written assignments**

1 Chronological	Description of a process or sequence
2 Classification	Categorising objects or ideas
3 Common denominator	Identification of a common characteristic or theme
4 Phased	Identification of short-/medium-/long-term aspects
5 Analytical	Examination of an issue in depth (situation - problem - solution - evaluation - recommendation)
6 Thematic	Comment on a theme in each aspect
7 Comparative/contrastive	Discussion of similarities and differences (often within a theme or themes)

be necessary to incorporate one of these models within another. For example, within the common denominator approach it may be necessary to include some chronological dimension to the discussion.

Examples of each of these seven approaches are given below.

Chronological approach

An example of the chronological approach would be describing a developmental process, such as outlining the historical development of the European Union. This kind of writing is most likely to be entirely descriptive.

Classification approach

An example of this approach could be to discuss transport by subdividing your text into land, sea and air modes of travel. Each of these could be further divided into commercial, military and personal modes of transport. These categories could be further subdivided on the basis of how they are powered. Such classifications are, to some extent, subjective, but the approach provides a means of describing each category at each level in a way that allows some contrast. This approach is particularly useful in scientific disciplines. The rationale also is sympathetic to the approach of starting from broad generalisation to the more specific.

Common denominator approach

An example of this approach might be used in answer to the following assignment: 'Account for the levels of high infant mortality in developing countries'. This suggests a common denominator of deficiency or lack. This topic could therefore be approached under the headings:

- Lack of primary health care
- Lack of health education
- Lack of literacy.

Phased approach

An example of adopting a sequential approach to a topic might be in answer to a task that instructs: 'Discuss the impact of water shortage on flora and fauna along river banks'.

- **Short-term factors** might be that drying out of the river bed occurs and annual plants fail to thrive.
- **Medium-term factors** might include damage to oxygenating plant life and reduction in wildlife numbers.
- **Long-term factors** might include the effect on the water table and falling numbers of certain amphibious species.

Note that topics amenable to this treatment do not always prompt this sort of response directly by asking for 'results' or consequences of an event; you could decide to use it in answer to a question such as 'Explain why water shortage has deleterious effects on riperian life.'

Analytical approach

This conventional approach might be used to approach complex issues. An example of an assignment that you could tackle in this way might be: 'Evaluate potential solutions to the problem of identity theft'. You could perhaps adopt the following plan:

- Define identity theft, and perhaps give an example.
- Explain why identity theft is difficult to control.
- Outline legal and practical solutions to identity theft.
- Weigh up the advantages and disadvantages of each.
- State which solution(s) you would favour and why.

---

smart tip

Adopting an analytical approach

This is particularly helpful in the construction of essays, reports, projects and case studies. It is also useful whenever you feel that you cannot identify themes or trends. This approach helps you to 'deconstruct' or 'unpack' the topic and involves five elements:

- **Situation:** describe the context and brief history.
- **Problem:** describe or define the problem.
- **Solution:** describe and explain the possible solution(s).
- **Evaluation:** identify the positive and negative features for each solution by giving evidence/reasons to support your viewpoint.
- **Recommendation:** identify the best option in your opinion, giving the basis of your reasoning for this. This element is optional, as it may not always be a requirement of your task.

Thematic approach

This approach is similar to the phased approach, but in this case themes are the identifying characteristics. Precise details would depend on the nature of the question, but possible examples could be:

- social, economic or political factors;
- age, income and health considerations;
- gas, electricity, oil, water and wind power.

Comparative/contrastive approach

This is a derivative of the themed approach. For example, consider a task that instructs: 'Discuss the arguments for and against the introduction of car-free city centres'. You might approach this by creating a 'grid', as in Table 9.2, which notes positive and negative aspects for the major stakeholders.

There are two potential methods of constructing text in this comparative/contrastive approach:

- **Method 1.** Introduce the topic, then follow Column A in a vertical fashion, then similarly follow Column B and conclude by making a concluding statement about the merits and demerits of one over the other. In relation to the grid, this would result in the structure: introductory statement, then A1 + A2 + A3 + A4 + A5, then B1 + B2 + B3 + B4 + B5, followed by concluding statement.

Table 9.2 **Model grid for planning comparison-type answers**

		Column A	Column B
	Stakeholders	Positive aspects	Negative aspects
1	Pedestrians	Greater safety, clean	Lengthy walk, poor parking
2	Drivers	Less stress; park and ride facilities	High parking fees; expensive public transport
3	Commercial enterprises	Quicker access for deliveries	Loss of trade to more accessible out-of-town shopping centres
4	Local authority	Reduces emissions	Cost of park and ride
5	Police	Easier to police	Reliance on foot patrols

- **Method 2.** Introduce the topic and than discuss the perspective of pedestrians from first the positive and then the negative aspects; now do the same for the viewpoints of the other stakeholders in sequence. This would result in the structure: introductory statement, then A1 + B1; A2 + B2; A3 + B3; A4 + B4; A5 + B5, followed by concluding statement.

Comparative/contrastive structures

Each method of structuring the points has advantages and disadvantages, according to the content and the context of the assignment. For example, in an exam it might be risky to embark on method 1 in case you run out of time and never reach the discussion of column B. In this instance, method 2 would enable a balanced answer.

→ Expanding your outline

Once you have decided what kind of approach is required to cover your written assignment, then you can map this on to the main body of your essay plan and frame an introduction and conclusion that will 'top and tail' the essay. In this way, you can create the outline plan based on the introduction–main body–conclusion model that provides the framework for academic writing (**Ch 8**) in the English-speaking world.

---

smart tip

Responding to question words

Not all tasks are based on instructions; some do ask questions. For instance, they may include words such as 'How ... ?', 'Why ... ?' and expressions such as 'To what extent ... ?' In these cases, you will need to think about what these mean within the do-describe-analyse-argue instruction hierarchy. One way to do this is to reword the question.

For example, consider the question: 'To what extent has the disposal of sewage effluence in rivers contributed to depletion of fish stocks over the last decade?'

This might be reworded as: 'Outline the relationship between the disposal of sewage effluence in rivers and the depletion of fish stocks over the last decade'.

This would suggest using a phased approach to organising the content of the answer to the question.

Practical tips for planning the outline of your written text

Return to the outline plan. When you have completed your first draft it is a good idea to go back to your outline plan and check that you have not forgotten any points. You can also make sure that the links between sections that you noted in the plan have been achieved.

Achieve balance in your response. Especially in the early years of university study, there is a tendency to adhere to the methods that had succeeded at school or college. This means that written work is often descriptive rather than analytical (see **Ch 7** for explanation). Ensure that the description you give is sufficient for the task, but if the instruction requires you to analyse or argue, then make sure this is the main focus of your response.

Explain your approach. Although the models outlined in this chapter are fairly standard approaches to tackling academic issues, it is still necessary to identify for your reader which approach you intend to adopt in the piece of text. Your reader should learn at an early point in your writing of the route you intend to follow. In most cases this would be in your introduction. This is dealt with more fully in **Ch 8**.

(GO) And now . . .

9.1 Compare textual patterns. Look at a chapter in a basic textbook and analyse the structural approach the author has taken. Identify the proportion of space allocated to 'scene-setting' using description, and to the analysis/argument/ evaluation components of the text.

9.2 Identify response types. Look at some of the essay titles or report assignments you have been set. Try to identify which of the approaches given in this chapter might best 'fit' each task.

9.3 Practise converting questions into instructions. If past exam papers' coursework exercises include tasks framed as questions, try converting them into instruction tasks and decide which type they fit into within the 'do-describe-analyse-argue' classification (**Ch 3**).

Writing technique

Academic writing style

How to adopt the appropriate language conventions

Writing for academic purposes is a vital skill, yet the stylistic codes you need to follow are rarely comprehensively defined. This chapter will help you understand what it means to write in an academic style and outlines some forms of language to avoid.

Key topics:

→ What is academic style?
→ Being objective
→ Appropriate use of tense
→ Use of appropriate vocabulary
→ Transforming non-academic to academic language

Key words

Acronym   Colloquial   Idiom   Noun   Phrasal verb   Pronoun   Register
Rhetorical question   Verb

University assignments can take several forms, such as an essay, a report, a project portfolio, a case study or a dissertation. One thing that is common to all these types of writing is that they need to follow academic style. While it is possible to identify differences between 'scientific' and 'humanities' styles in the finer detail, this chapter covers the common features of all types of academic writing.

→ What is academic style?

Academic style involves the use of precise and objective language to express ideas. It must be grammatically correct, and is more formal than the style used in novels, newspapers, informal correspondence and everyday conversation. This should mean that the language is clear and simple. It does not imply that it is complex, pompous and dry. Above all, academic style is *objective*, using language techniques that generally maintain an impersonal tone and a vocabulary that is more succinct, rather than involving personal, colloquial, or idiomatic expressions.

British English (BE) versus American English (AE)

Academic writing in the UK nearly always adopts BE. The differences are most evident in spelling; for example, 'colour' (BE) and 'color' (AE). However, there are also differences in vocabulary, so that in AE people talk of 'professor' for 'lecturer'; and in language use, so that in AE someone might write 'we have gotten results', rather than 'we have obtained results'. In some disciplines, there is an attempt at standardisation, for example, in chemistry the spelling of 'sulphur' (BE) has become 'sulfur' (AE) as the international standard.

→ Being objective

When writing academically, it is important that your personal involvement with your topic does not overshadow the importance of what you are commenting on or reporting. The main way of demonstrating this lack of bias is by using impersonal language. This means:

- Avoiding personal pronouns – try not to use the following words:

  I/me/one

  you (singular and plural)

  we/us.

- Using the passive rather than active voice – try to write about the action and not about the actor (the person who performed the action – see below).

You can use other strategies to maintain an impersonal style in your writing. For general statements, you could use a structure such as 'it is . . .', 'there is . . .' or 'there are . . .' to introduce sentences. For more specific points relating to statements you have already made, you could use the structures 'this is . . .' or 'these are . . .'; 'that is . . .' or 'those are . . .' with appropriate tense changes according to the context. Don't forget that when you use words like 'it', 'this', 'these', 'that' or 'those', there should be no ambiguity over the word or phrase to which they refer.

Another way in which you can maintain objectivity by writing impersonally is to change the verb in the sentence to a noun and then reframe the sentence in a less personal way.

We **applied** pressure to the wound to stem bleeding (*verb in bold*).
The **application** of pressure stemmed bleeding (*noun in bold*).

This kind of text-juggling will become second nature as you tackle more and more assignments.

Passive and active voice

This is best explained from examples:

- Pressure was applied to the wound to stem bleeding (passive).
- We applied pressure to the wound to stem bleeding (active).

Some would argue that the second example is clearer, but their opponents would counter-argue that the use of 'we' takes attention away from the action.

You may find that the grammar checkers in some word-processing packages suggest that passive expressions should be changed to active. However, if you follow this guidance, you will find yourself having to use a personal pronoun, which is inconsistent with impersonal academic style. If in doubt, ask your tutors for their preference.

→ Appropriate use of tense

The past tense is used in academic writing to describe or comment on things that have already happened. However, there are times when the present tense is appropriate. For example, in a report you might write 'Figure 5 shows . . .', rather than 'Figure 5 showed . . .', when describing your results. A material and methods section, on the other hand, will always be·in the past tense, because it describes what you *did*.

In colloquial English, there is often a tendency to misuse tenses. This can creep into academic assignments, especially where the author is narrating a sequence of events.

The following examples illustrate two ways of writing a paragraph using different tenses:

Napoleon **orders** his troops to advance on Moscow. The severe winter **closes** in on them and they **come back** a ragbag of an army. (Present tense in bold.)

and:

Napoleon **ordered** his troops to advance on Moscow. The severe winter **closed** in on them and they **came back** a ragbag of an army. (Simple past tense in bold.)

While the first of these examples might work with the soundtrack of a documentary on Napoleon's Russian campaign, it is too colloquial for academic written formats.

Plain English

There has been a growing movement in recent times that advocates the use of 'plain English', and it has been very successful in persuading government departments and large commercial organisations to simplify written material for public reference. This has been achieved by introducing a less formal style of language that uses simpler, more active sentence structures, and a simpler range of vocabulary avoiding jargon. This is an admirable development. However, academic writing style needs to be precise, professional and unambiguous, and the strategies of 'plain English' campaigners may not be entirely appropriate to the style expected of you as an academic author. For the same reasons, some of the suggestions offered by software packages may be inappropriate to your subject and academic conventions.

→ Use of appropriate vocabulary

Good academic writers think carefully about their choice of words. The 'plain English' movement (see above) recommends that words of Latin origin should be replaced by their Anglo-Saxon, or spoken, alternatives. However, this does not always contribute to the style and precision appropriate to academic authorship. For example, compare:

If we **turn down** the volume, then there will be no feedback.

and

> If we *turn down* the offer from the World Bank, then interest rates will rise.

Both sentences make sense, but they use the two-word verb 'turn down' in different senses. These verbs are properly called phrasal verbs and they often have more than a single meaning. Furthermore, they are also used more in speech than in formal writing. Therefore, it would be better to write:

> If we *reduce* the volume, then there will be no feedback.

and

> If we *reject* the offer from the World Bank, then interest rates will rise.

By using 'reduce' and 'reject' the respective meanings are clear, concise and unambiguous. If you are restricted to a word limit on your work, using the one-word verb has additional obvious advantages. Table 12.2 gives you the chance to explore some further two-word verbs and their one-word equivalents. **Ch 15** explores other areas of vocabulary usage and development.

Non-sexist language

The Council of Europe recommends that, where possible, gender-specific language is avoided. Thus: 'S/he will provide specimens for her/his exam'. This is rather clumsy, but, by transforming the sentence into the plural, this is avoided: 'They will provide specimens for their exams'.

Alternatively, if appropriate, 'you/your' could be used.

→ Transforming non-academic to academic language

Thinking about the style of your writing should be a feature of any review you make of drafts of your written work (**Ch 16**). Table 10.1 gives a specific example of text conversion from informal to formal style. Table 10.2 provides several pointers to help you achieve a more academic style.

The common errors of language use to avoid in your writing are:

- poor grammar (**Ch 12**);
- imprecise, woolly wording (**Ch 15**);
- use of personal pronouns (p. 106);
- colloquial language, such as idiom, slang and cliché (Table 10.2);
- absolute terms, when inappropriate (Table 10.2);
- value judgements (**Ch 7**); and
- easily rectified mistakes, such as spelling and punctuation errors (**Ch 13** and **Ch 14**).

Table 10.1 Example of converting a piece of 'non-academic' writing into academic style. Note that the conversion results in a slightly longer piece of text (47 versus 37 words). This emphasises the point that while you should aim for concise writing, precise wording may be more important.

Original text (non-academic style)	'Corrected' text (academic style)
In this country, we have changed the law so that the King or Queen is less powerful since the Great War. But he or she can still advise, encourage or warn the Prime Minister if they want.	In the United Kingdom, legislation has been a factor in the decline of the role of the monarchy in the period since the Great War. Nevertheless, the monarchy has survived and, thus, the monarch continues to exercise the right to advise, encourage and warn the Prime Minister.
Points needing correction	**Corrected points**
• Non-specific wording (*this country*)	• Specific wording (country specified: *in the United Kingdom*)
• Personal pronoun (*we*)	• Impersonal language (*legislation has*)
• Weak grammar (*but* is a connecting word and should not be used to start a sentence).	• Appropriate signpost word (*nevertheless*)
• Word with several meanings (*law*)	• Generic, yet well-defined term (*legislation*)
• Duplication of nouns (*king or queen*)	• Singular abstract term (*monarchy*)
• Inconsistent and potentially misleading pronoun use (*he or she, they*)	• Repeated subject (*monarch*) and reconstructed sentence
• Informal style (*can still*)	• More formal style (*continues to exercise*)

Table 10.2 Fundamentals of academic writing. These elements of academic writing are laid out in alphabetical order. Being aware of these and training yourself to follow them will help you to develop as an academic author and will ensure that you don't lose marks by making some basic errors of usage or expression.

Abbreviations and acronyms

It is acceptable to use abbreviations in academic writing to express units, for example, SI units. Otherwise, abbreviations are generally reserved for note-taking. Thus, avoid: e.g. (for example), i.e. (that is), viz. (namely) in formal work.

Acronyms are a kind of abbreviation formed by taking the initial letters of a name of an organisation, a procedure or an apparatus, and then using these letters instead of writing out the title in full. Thus, World Health Organisation becomes WHO. The academic convention is that the first time that you use a title with an acronym alternative, then you should write it in full with the acronym in brackets immediately after the full title. Thereafter, within that document you can use the acronym. For example:

The European Free Trade Association (EFTA) has close links with the European Community (EC). Both EFTA and the EC require new members to have membership of the Council of Europe as a prerequisite for admission to their organisations.

In some forms of academic writing, for example formal reports, you may be expected to include a list of abbreviations in addition to these first-time-of-use explanations.

'Absolute' terms

In academic writing, it is important to be cautious about using absolute terms such as:

always and **never; most** and **all; least** and **none.**

This does not prevent you from using these words; it simply means that they should be used with caution, that is, when you are absolutely certain of your ground.

Clichés

Living languages change and develop over time. This means that some expressions come into such frequent usage that they lose their meaning; indeed, they can often be replaced with a much less long-winded expression. For example:

First and foremost (first); **last but not least** (finally); **at this point in time** (now).

This procedure is the **gold standard** of hip replacement methods.
(This procedure is the best hip replacement method.)

In the second example, 'gold standard' is completely inappropriate; correctly used, it should refer to monetary units, but it has been misused by being introduced into other contexts.

►

Table 10.2 continued

Colloquial language
This term encompasses informal language that is common in speech. Colloquialisms and idiomatic language should not be used in academic writing. This example shows how colloquial language involving cliché and idiom has been misused: **Not to beat about the bush,** increasing income tax did the Chancellor **no good at the end of the day** and he **was ditched** at the next Cabinet reshuffle. (Increasing income tax did not help the Chancellor and he was replaced at the next Cabinet reshuffle.)
'Hedging' language
For academic purposes, it is often impossible to state categorically that something is or is not the case. There are verbs that allow you to 'hedge your bets' by not coming down on one side or another of an argument, or which allow you to present a variety of different scenarios without committing yourself to any single position. **seems that   looks as if   suggests that   appears that.** This involves using a language construction that leaves the reader with the sense that the evidence presented is simply supporting a hypothetical, or imaginary, case. To emphasise this sense of 'hedging', the use of a special kind of verb is introduced. These modal verbs are: **can/cannot   could/could not   may/may not   might/might not.** These can be used with a variety of other verbs to increase the sense of tentativeness. For example: These results **suggest** that there has been a decline in herring stocks in the North Sea. Even more tentatively, this could be: These results **could suggest** that there has been a decline in herring stocks in the North Sea.
Jargon and specialist terms
Most subjects make use of language in a way that is exclusive to that discipline. It is important, therefore, to explain terms that a general reader might not understand. It is always good practice to define specialist terms or 'regular' words that are being used in a very specific way.
Rhetorical questions
Some writers use direct rhetorical questions as a stylistic vehicle to introduce the topic addressed by the question. This is a good strategy if you are making a speech and it can have some power in academic writing, although it should be used sparingly. Example: **How do plants survive in dry weather?** a rhetorical question, could be rephrased as: **It is important to understand how plants survive in dry weather.** (Note: no question mark needed.)

Table 10.2 continued

Split infinitives
The most commonly quoted split infinitive comes from the TV series *Star Trek* where Captain James T. Kirk states that the aim of the Star Ship Enterprise is 'to boldly go where no man has gone before'. This means that an adverb (boldly) has split the infinitive (to go). It should read as 'to go boldly'. Many traditionalists consider that the split infinitive is poor English, although modern usage increasingly ignores the rule. Nevertheless, it is probably better to avoid the split infinitive in academic writing, which tends to be particularly traditional.

Value judgements
These are defined as statements in which the author or speaker is imposing their views or values on to the reader. For example, a writer who states that 'Louis XIV was a rabid nationalist' without giving supporting evidence for this statement is not making an objective comment in a professional manner. Rewording this statement to: 'Louis XIV was regarded as a rabid nationalist. This is evident in the nature of his foreign policy where he . . .' offers the reader some evidence that explains the claim (see p. 80).

Practical tips for ensuring that you write in an academic style

Think about your audience. Your readers should direct the style you adopt for any writing you do. For example, if you were writing to your bank manager asking for a loan, you would not use text-messaging or informal language. Similarly, for academic writing, you should take into account that your reader(s) will probably be marking your work and, in addition to knowledge and content, they will be looking for evidence of awareness and correct use of specialist terms and structures.

Avoid contractions. In spoken English, shortened forms such as, *don't, can't, isn't, it's, I'd* and *we'll* are used all the time. However, in academic written English, they should not be used. Texting contractions are also inappropriate.

Avoid personal pronouns. Experiment with other language structures so that you avoid the personal pronouns, *I/me/one, you* and *we/us*, and their possessive forms, *my, your* and *our*.

10.1 Take steps to improve your writing style. Correct English is essential in academic writing. **Ch 12** presents points about grammar that may apply to your work. Look at Table 12.2 in order to understand the grammatical terms first, and then look at the contrasting samples of student writing in Table 12.1. Highlight points that you do not know at present and resolve to use this information in your written work. You may be able to find errors that your lecturers have identified in feedback on your work. Next, consult a grammar book (see p. 133) to find out more about the relevant grammar point. You can consolidate your understanding by doing the exercises provided in such books.

10.2 Ask a friend to work with you on your writing style. Swap a piece of writing and check over your friend's writing and ask them to do the same for yours. When you have done this, compare the points you have found. Try to explain what you think could be improved. Together, you may be able to clarify some aspects that you were unaware were problematic. Afterwards look at **Ch 12** and follow the suggestion in point 10.1 above.

10.3 Learn from published academic writing in your discipline. Look at a textbook or journal article – especially in the area that discusses results or evidence or recommendations. Try to find examples of the use of 'hedging' language (Table 10.2) and note what else authors do with language in order to ensure that they avoid making absolute judgements.

11 | Shaping your text

How to create effective sentences and paragraphs

When is a sentence not a sentence? What makes a paragraph? These are questions that often arise for students as academic authors. Sentences can sometimes be too short, too long, or poorly structured – and the same can be said of paragraphs. If you are not sure why any of this is the case, then this chapter explains what makes a good sentence and a paragraph that is cohesive and conveys information coherently.

Key topics:

→ What is a sentence?
→ What is a paragraph?

Key terms
Clause   Subject   Subordinate clause   Verb

Knowing how sentences and paragraphs are structured and how you can produce good, clear sentences will help a great deal in shaping a piece of academic text, whether it is for an essay, a report, a dissertation or another kind of assignment. It is important to recognise that academic writing does not mean constructing long and involved sentences full of impressive-sounding 'big' words. Sometimes short sentences have more impact because they are brief and simple. If there is a rule to remember here, it is write to express, not to impress.

There are many excellent grammar books available to give detailed explanations and exercises on the mechanics of academic writing (p. 133). In this chapter we aim to give only some of the basic information on sentence and paragraph construction. Experience indicates that students want to know why what they have written is wrong and so, by providing a little background understanding and some models that show some typical problems, we hope to help you to be more sentence- and paragraph-aware when you write, craft and review your own writing.

Writers' tip

Reading a sentence aloud can be a useful way of deciding whether a sentence you have written works well and is grammatically correct. Your ears will perhaps make more (non)sense out of it than your eyes.

→ What is a sentence?

A sentence must have a verb, that is, a 'doing' word (**Ch 12**). Each of the following is a sentence (verb in bold):

Help!

Students **work** in the holidays.

Universities **provide** tuition in a wide range of subjects.

Simple sentences

These have at least a *subject* (the person or thing doing the action) and a **verb**, sometimes followed by a phrase of other information. Together these make sense as a unit. For example:

Criminal Law **differs** from Civil Law.

Plants **require** sunlight and water.

Divalent ions **carry** two charges.

Compound sentences

These are two simple sentences joined by **and** or **but**. There will be two verbs in this combined sentence. For example:

Scots Law and English Law are fundamentally different, **but** there are some areas in which they are similar.

Complex sentences

These sentences consist of a main clause with additional subordinate clauses. A clause is a unit of meaning built round a verb. There are two categories of clause: principal (sometimes called independent or main clause, which is like a simple sentence) and subordinate clauses. The subordinate clause contains a verb, but would not make sense if it were to stand alone. It does the work of an adjective, adverb or noun.

'Dangling phrases'

Dangling phrases do not make sentences:

Bringing the debate to an end.

Having been at war for 100 years.

Gum trees **being** susceptible to termite infestation.

The bold words denote dangling phrases. They do contain verbs, but these are only in participle form ('–ing' words, see Table 12.2 and Figure 15.2) and not fully formed verbs such as 'differs', 'require' and 'carry' in the sentences above formed correctly. The use of such dangling phrases is common in student essays. Here is a correct version of a sentence that uses a participle phrase. In this case, the participle phrase needs to relate to the subject of the main clause (both shown in bold):

The **countries** of Europe, **having been at war for 100 years**, were financially exhausted.

The following are examples of subordinate clauses (shown in bold):

Gait analysis gives insights into the walking difficulties **that are experienced by people with cerebral palsy.**

Social work legislation protects the rights of the elderly **when they are no longer able to cope independently.**

Although Britain is regarded as a democracy, it has no written constitution **that can be cited as the basis of Constitutional Law.**

Complex sentences can be quite long and can contain more than one subordinate clause. Varying the length of your sentences enlivens your text and helps to keep your reader's interest. However, shorter sentences containing a single idea generally have a stronger impact than longer complex sentences. If you want to balance two ideas, then compound sentences are best.

Models for academic writing: what to avoid

Newspaper journalism and layout favours paragraphs of single sentences, but these are not good models for academic writing. Similarly, adopting a flowery or pompous style is not appropriate to academic writing. See **Ch 10** for further tips.

→ What is a paragraph?

A paragraph is a unit of text usually comprising several sentences. It has a topic that is outlined in the first sentence; the topic is developed further within the paragraph; and the paragraph concludes with a sentence that terminates that topic or, possibly, acts as a link to the topic of the following paragraph.

Paragraph and structure

The building blocks of paragraphs are sentences, each performing a particular role: as detailed in Table 11.1, and seen in action within the example shown in Figure 11.1. This example is a very straightforward listing paragraph.

Table 11.2 gives examples of signpost, or linking, words that you can use to join the component sentences within a paragraph so that your text flows smoothly and Table 11.3 provides a range of different paragraph models.

How should I lay out my paragraphs? **?**

This can follow a 'blocked' style or an indented style **Ch 19**. It is normal to leave space between blocked paragraphs so that readers recognise that there is a change in topic. The general rule is to leave a single line space.

Table 11.1 **Some types of sentences that are used to make up a paragraph**

Type of sentence	Role in the paragraph
Topic introducer sentence	Introduces the overall topic of the text (generally in the very first paragraph)
Topic sentence	Introduces a paragraph by identifying the topic of that paragraph
Developer sentence	Expands the topic by giving additional information
Modulator sentence	Acts as linking sentence and is often introduced by a signpost word moving to another aspect of the topic within the same paragraph
Terminator sentence	Concludes the discussion of a topic within a paragraph, but can also be used as a **transition sentence** where it provides a link to the topic of the next paragraph

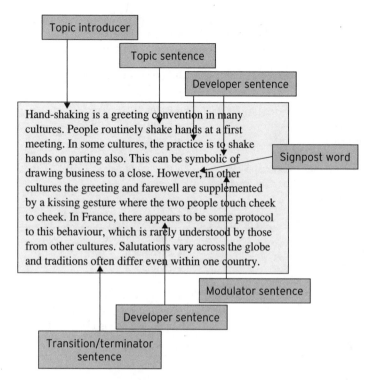

Figure 11.1 How sentences make up a paragraph. Part of a text on Anthropology, showing how different types of sentences are used to construct a paragraph.

Table 11.2 Signpost words in text. This table provides examples of words and phrases that can be used to improve the flow of your writing.

Type of link intended	Examples of signpost words
Addition	additionally; furthermore; in addition; moreover
Cause/reason	as a result of; because (mid-sentence)
Comparison	compared with; in the same way; in comparison with; likewise
Condition	if; on condition that; providing that; unless
Contrast	although; by contrast; conversely; despite; however; nevertheless; yet
Effect/result	as a result; hence; therefore; thus
Exemplification	for example; for instance; particularly; such as; thus
Reformulation	in other words; rather; to paraphrase
Summary	finally; hence; in all; in conclusion; in short; in summary
Time sequence	after; at first; at last; before; eventually; subsequently
Transition	as far as . . . is concerned; as for; to turn to

Table 11.3 Paragraph models. The construction of paragraph types is modelled under each heading. The numbers of intermediate sentences of each type is arbitrary – you could use more or fewer according to the need or context.

Describing: appearance/position	Describing: time sequence
• Topic introducer • Developer 1 • Developer 2 • Developer 3 • Terminator sentence Descriptive sequence examples: top to bottom; left to right; centre to perimeter	Either: • Event 1 • Event 2 • Event 3 Or: • By date order
Describing: process – how it works	**Defining**
• Topic introducer • Developer 1 • Developer 2 . . . • Modulator • Developer 1 • Developer 2 . . . • Topic sentence	• Topic sentence • Example 1 • Example 2 • Example 3 • Terminator sentence Note: Don't use a different *form* of the word being defined in order to define it
Classifying	**Generalising**
• Topic sentence • Example 1 • Example 2 . . . • Terminator sentence identifying category	• Developer 1 • Developer 2 . . . • Topic sentence; generalisation Or: • Generalisation • Developer 1 • Developer 2 . . . • Restatement sentence
Giving examples	**Listing**
• Topic sentence • Example 1 • Example 2 . . . • Restatement sentence or terminator sentence	• Topic sentence • Developer sentence • Modulator sentence • Developer sentence • Terminator sentence
Relating cause and effect: method 1	**Relating cause and effect: method 2**
• Topic introducer • Topic sentence • Developer 1 • Developer 2 • Modulator • Developer 3 • Developer 4 • Terminator/restatement sentence	• Topic introducer • Topic sentence • Developer 1 Theme A • Developer 2 Theme A • Modulator (transfer to B) • Developer 1 Theme B • Developer 2 Theme B • Terminator/restatement sentence

Table 11.3 continued

Comparing	Contrasting
• Topic introducer	• Topic introducer
• Topic sentence	• Topic sentence
• Developer 1 Theme A	• Developer 1 Theme A
• Developer 2 Theme A ...	• Developer 1 Theme B
• Modulator (transfer to B)	• Developer 2 Theme A
• Developer 1 Theme B	• Developer 2 Theme B ...
• Developer 2 Theme B ...	• Terminator
• Restatement sentence	• Restatement sentence

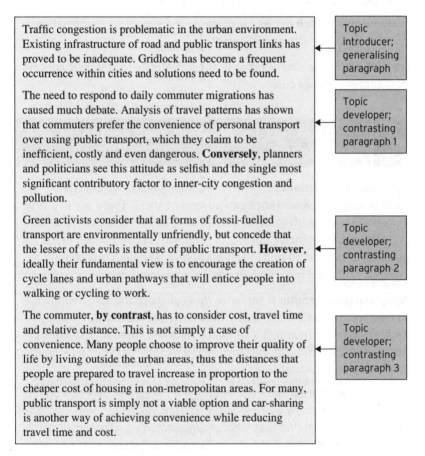

Traffic congestion is problematic in the urban environment. Existing infrastructure of road and public transport links has proved to be inadequate. Gridlock has become a frequent occurrence within cities and solutions need to be found.

Topic introducer; generalising paragraph

The need to respond to daily commuter migrations has caused much debate. Analysis of travel patterns has shown that commuters prefer the convenience of personal transport over using public transport, which they claim to be inefficient, costly and even dangerous. **Conversely**, planners and politicians see this attitude as selfish and the single most significant contributory factor to inner-city congestion and pollution.

Topic developer; contrasting paragraph 1

Green activists consider that all forms of fossil-fuelled transport are environmentally unfriendly, but concede that the lesser of the evils is the use of public transport. **However**, ideally their fundamental view is to encourage the creation of cycle lanes and urban pathways that will entice people into walking or cycling to work.

Topic developer; contrasting paragraph 2

The commuter, **by contrast**, has to consider cost, travel time and relative distance. This is not simply a case of convenience. Many people choose to improve their quality of life by living outside the urban areas, thus the distances that people are prepared to travel increase in proportion to the cheaper cost of housing in non-metropolitan areas. For many, public transport is simply not a viable option and car-sharing is another way of achieving convenience while reducing travel time and cost.

Topic developer; contrasting paragraph 3

Figure 11.2 How paragraphs make up a piece of text. Part of an essay on town planning, showing how different paragraphs have been used to construct a flowing piece of text. Note how the emboldened signpost words (Table 11.2) have been used.

If the building blocks of paragraphs are sentences, then paragraphs themselves are the building blocks of text. Each paragraph performs a particular role in the structure of text. This means that the examples of paragraph formats shown in Table 11.3 can be used to construct extended written text. The example in Figure 11.2 shows how paragraphs flow within a piece of text.

Deductive and inductive paragraph models

These are alternative methods of laying out an argument:

- **Deductive model:** the writer moves from the key point and follows it with supporting information or evidence.
- **Inductive model:** the writer presents the supporting information and concludes with the key point.

You might choose one or other of these methods to suit your context and content of your topic.

Practical tips for creating good sentences and paragraphs

How long is a sentence? This is a 'how long is a piece of string?' type of question. A sentence can be long or short. There are two tests for good sentence structure. First, simply read it out aloud. Your ear will hear inconsistencies of logic or grammar. Second, if you feel a need to take a breath in mid-sentence, then a comma is probably needed, or even a full stop followed by a new sentence.

Vary sentence length. A sentence 'mix' of short and long sentences is probably more reader-friendly than lines and lines of unbroken text. As a rule of thumb, if a sentence runs into three or four lines of typescript, then consider restructuring it in some way or breaking it up into two smaller sentences.

How long is a paragraph? The length of a paragraph depends on the content, but generally extra-long paragraphs will have some topic shift within them. If you find that your paragraph seems disproportionately long, then, again, read it aloud and listen for a 'natural' break point. This is probably a good place to start a new paragraph.

Use signpost words. These words are used to assist your reader by moving them through the logic of your text, for example, in modulator sentences. Some words are most frequently used at the beginning of sentences: for example, however, moreover, furthermore, nevertheless. These are followed by a comma and then the point you wish to make.

(GO) And now . . .

11.1 Take tips from the professionals. Select a short section from a textbook. Analyse a couple of paragraphs, looking, in particular, for the introducers, developers, modulators (and signpost words) and transition/terminator sentences. Now select text from a piece of your own writing and do the same thing. How balanced is the paragraph structure? Have you overused or underused signpost words?

11.2 Assess your own writing for clarity of meaning.
Continuing with your own text, check for clarity and conciseness. Have you used any dangling phrases (non-sentences)? Have you used simple or compound sentences too often? Are your complex sentences perhaps too complex? Are there too many subordinate clauses? Could some overlong sentences be modified to become simple or compound sentences?

11.3 Look at Ch 13 on punctuation. There are tips on how to use commas, colons and semicolons in extended writing. These punctuation marks are important in breaking up ideas in text into paragraphs and sentences. With this information beside you, look critically at your own writing. Try to spot places where it might be helpful to your reader if you modified the punctuation to make your sentences and paragraphs clearer and unambiguous.

12 | Improving your grammar

How to avoid some common errors

Many people, not just students, often state that they don't know much about the grammar of English – but what exactly do they mean? Spelling? Sentence structure? Parts of speech? Tense? Word order? The list seems to be endless. This chapter takes a quick look at some common mistakes and tries to provide enough in the way of grammatical terms to allow you to understand the guidance on electronic grammar checkers or in the feedback you receive on your assignments.

Key topics:
→ Why grammar is important
→ Common grammatical errors
→ How to use grammar checkers to best advantage

Key terms
Clause   Preposition   Tautology   Tense

Grammar is the series of rules that governs the use of any language. It is a vast field and, although intuitively people know many of the 'rules' of grammar when speaking, it is often less easy to apply them in writing. This chapter cannot provide a complete set of rules, but gives you enough information to enable you to find what you need in a specialist grammar book or in a standard dictionary.

→ Why grammar is important

Grammar is important to you as a student because it is an integral and expected component of academic writing. Good grammar is essential, because without it your writing may be nonsensical, illogical or ambiguous. In the course of your university studies you will come across many aspects of language where you need to know exactly how the appropriate grammar rule needs to be applied.

In the past, there have been two approaches to teaching grammar. The traditional approach teaches the 'technical' terms, for example, 'clause', 'preposition' and 'tense', so that these can be used to explain the mechanics of language; the other, modern, approach encourages people to write freely and then provides them feedback with correct models. For the purposes of this book, we shall use elements of both techniques because we believe that some people do want to know the 'proper grammar', but, at the same time, they may learn best by seeing models of how this works in practice. So, we'll show you some of the more common grammatical errors and explain these as simply as possible, using the grammatical terms only where absolutely necessary.

If you are eager for more information, then you may find it helpful to look at **Ch 10** on academic style, **Ch 13** on punctuation, **Ch 14** on spelling and **Ch 15** on vocabulary. These elements are all interdependent in the production of good style, structure and grammar in academic writing.

→ Common grammatical errors

There are many common errors that occur in academic writing. Table 12.1 demonstrates how grammatical errors in a weak style of writing can be corrected to produce a more academic form of writing. In order to understand comments or corrections on your written work, it may be helpful to be able to identify some grammar terms. Table 12.2 defines and explains some of the terms you may come across. Table 12.3 gives some examples of errors and their corrections. Highlighting those that could be helpful to you in your writing will help you to create a personal checklist so you can avoid mistakes in future.

Grammatical terms

Grammar has its own particular terminology. This is used as a shorthand reference to allow discussion of more complex ideas. It's rather like the way that knowing the names of the main parts of a car engine helps you to understand the explanation of the mechanic who's fixing your car. The most common grammar terms are given in a very simplified form in Table 12.2. If you can become familiar with some of the basic terms, then this may help you to understand comments written on your assignments. This will also help you when looking up the relevant section in a good grammar book, when you think this might be useful.

Table 12.1 Comparison of weak and strong academic writing. This text is part of an answer to the question: 'Did Napoleon achieve most for France at home or abroad?' The original answer, written in a style that is essentially non-academic, is in the left column. The right-hand column is a key to some of the grammatical weaknesses in the use of language, and the final section of the table provides one possible example of how the same text could be written in a more academic style.

Non-academic style (bold text indicates error)	Error and correction analysis
Napolion[1] *came up trumps*[2] *in both French domestic and foreign policies that were **many and varied**.*[3] *How **you have to think about**[4] the value of these achievements is **the million dollar question**.*[5] *While his domestic reforms survived after his **collapse**,*[6] *most of the **affects**[7] of his foreign policy necessarily perished with his imperial power. In addition **to this**,*[8] *the value of his achievements has to be considered in the light of whether they were achievements for France or achievements in consolidating his own position and popularity.* **In this essay I will talk about**[9] *his foreign and domestic policys.*[10]	1 Misspelling of key name
	2, 3 Clichés
	4 Personal expression;
	5 Cliché/inappropriate language
	6 Ambiguous
	7 Misspelling
	8 Unnecessary words (phrase not used in corrected version)
	9 Statement of intent: use of personal pronouns – and you cannot 'talk' on paper!
	10 Misspelling
*In foreign policy, Napoleon's primary achievement was the Peace of Lunéville (1801) with Austria and subsequent Treaty of Amiens with Britain in 1802. This achievement was significant '**cos**[12] it gave both France and Napoleon, **not to mention**[13] their antagonists, a **breathing space**[14] in which to collect **there**[15] resources and reorganise themselves for further hostilities. This initial **bargain**[16] enabled Napoleon **to have a look at**[17] the domestic state of France after a decade of almost continuous international **squabbling**[18] following a major internal political revolution. **Applying the same methods to the affairs of state as he did to the tactics of the battlefield.**[19] In **both two**[20] ways he had to take into consideration the outlook and demands of the French people as a **hole**.[21] This approach he took on **the grounds that**[22] 'I act only on the imagination of the nation. When this means fails me, I shall be reduced to nothing and another will succeed me.'[23]*	11 Add transition sentence to new version to link topic sentence with preceding paragraph
	12 Shortened word (not used in corrected version)
	13 Unnecessary words
	14 Informal language
	15 Misspelling
	16 More appropriate word required
	17 Too informal
	18 More appropriate word required
	19 Incomplete sentence/phrase (hanging participle)
	20 Tautology (same meaning twice)
	21 Misspelling;
	22 Wordy cliché
	23 No reference cited: Harvard method citation added

Academic style (bold text indicates correction/addition)

Napoleon's[1] **achievements**[2] in both French domestic and foreign policies **were significant**.[3] However, **the relative merit of these achievements must be considered**[4,5] at two levels. Firstly, although his domestic reforms survived his **downfall**,[6] most of the **effects**[7] of his foreign policy necessarily perished with his imperial power. **Secondly,**[8] the extent to which his achievements were truly for the greater glory of France or were simply strategies for consolidating his own position and popularity has to be taken into account. **The purpose of this essay**[9] **will be to evaluate these two dimensions within his foreign and domestic policies**[10] **in the longer term.**

Table 12.1 continued

> **Domestic and foreign policy in this period cannot easily be separated. In foreign policy,**[11] Napoleon's primary achievement was the Peace of Lunéville (1801) with Austria and subsequent Treaty of Amiens with Britain in 1802. The significance of this achievement was that it gave both France and Napoleon, **and their antagonists,**[13] **an interval**[14] in which to collect **their**[15] resources and reorganise themselves for further hostilities. This initial **accord**[16] enabled Napoleon to **survey**[17] the domestic state of France after a decade of almost continuous **fighting**[18] preceded by a major internal political revolution. **He applied the same methods to the affairs of state as he did to the tactics of the battlefield;**[19] in **both**[20] he had to take into consideration the outlook and demands of the French people as a **whole.**[21] This approach he took **because**[22] 'I act only on the imagination of the nation. When this means fails me, I shall be reduced to nothing and another will succeed me' **(Grant and Temperley, 1952).**[23]

Table 12.2 Grammar toolkit: definitions to help you seek more information

Grammar term	Definition/model	Example
Adjective	Describes nouns or gerunds.	A **red** book; an **innovative** project.
Adverb	Adds information as to how something is done.	The student read **quickly**.
Articles	There are only three in English: a, an, the. There are particular rules about using these and you will find these rules in a grammar book.	**A** shot in the dark. **An** empty house. **The** Highway Code.
Clause	Part of sentence containing a verb. If the verb and the words relating to it can stand alone, then they comprise the main clause. If the words cannot stand alone, then the verb and the words that go with it form a subordinate clause.	**Cats eat mice** which are vermin. *Main* *Subordinate* *clause* *clause*
Conditional	Used to explain a future possible situation; note the comma after the condition.	If I had the time, I **would go out**. *Condition* **Consequence**
Conjunction	Word that joins two clauses in a sentence where the ideas are connected or equally balanced.	The book was on loan **and** the student had to reserve it.
Demonstrative	There are four in English: this, these, that, those (see Table 12.3).	**This** house supports the abolition of smoking in public.
Direct object	The noun or pronoun that is affected by the verb.	Foxes kill **sheep**. Foxes eat **them**.

▶

Table 12.2 continued

Grammar term	Definition/model	Example
Future tense	Explaining things that have not yet happened. There are two forms: will/shall, going to.	I **shall work** until I am 65. They **will** come early. He **is going to** work harder.
Gerund	The gerund acts as a noun and is formed with the part of the verb called the present participle: ... **-ing**.	**Speaking** is easier than **writing** for most people.
Indirect object	The person or thing that benefits from the action of a verb.	Tutors give (to) **students** written work. They give (to) **them** essays.
Infinitive	Sometimes called the simple or root form of the verb. This form is usually listed in dictionaries, but without 'to'.	**To work.**
Noun	Term used to refer to things or people. There are different types: e.g. abstract (non-visible), concrete (visible) and proper nouns (names of people, places organisations, rivers, mountain ranges).	**Abstract noun:** thought. **Concrete nouns:** chair, table. **Proper nouns:** Caesar, Rome, the Post Office, the Rhine, the Andes (always begin with capitals).
Passive voice	Used to describe things objectively, that is, placing the emphasis of the sentence on the action rather than the actor. Although some electronic grammar checkers imply that the passive is wrong, it is perfectly correct. Often used in academic writing.	**Essays are written** by students. *Action Actor*
Past participle	This is usually formed by adding **-ed** to the verb stem. However, in English there are many irregular verbs (see 'tense', below). You will find lists of these verbs in many dictionaries.	**Worked.** However, there are many irregular verbs: e.g. bent, drunk; eaten, seen; thought; understood.
Present participle	This is formed by adding **-ing** to the simple verb form. It is used to form continuous verb tenses.	The sun is **setting**. We were **watching** the yachts.
Phrasal verb	These are two- or three-word verbs made up of a verb plus a particle (similar to a preposition). These verbs are generally regarded as being less formal in tone than single-word verbs.	**Set down** (deposit). **Pick up** (collect). **Write down** (note). **Look out for** (observe).

Table 12.2 continued

Grammar term	Definition/model	Example
Possessive	Word indicating ownership: my, mine, your, yours, his, her, its, our, ours, their, theirs.	My house and **his** are worth the same. **Mine** is larger but **his** has more land.
Preposition	Word used as a link relating verbs to nouns, pronouns and noun phrases. Sometimes these are followed by an article, sometimes not: at, by, in, for, from, of, on, over, through, under, with.	Put money **in** the bank **for** a rainy day or save it **for** summer holidays **in** the sun.
Pronoun	Word used instead of nouns: I, me, you, he, him, she, her, it, we, us, they, them. Also words such as: each, everyone.	I have given **it** to **him**.
Relative pronoun	Words that link adjective (describing) clauses to the noun about which they give more information: that, which, who, whose, whom.	This is the house **that** Jack built. Jack, **who** owns it, lives there. Jack, **whose** wife sings, is a baker. Jack, **to whom** we sold the flour, used it to bake a loaf.
Sentence	A grouping of words, one of which must be a verb, that can stand together independently and make sense.	The people elect their leaders in a democracy.
Subject	The person or thing that performs the action in a sentence.	**Caesar** invaded Britain. **Caterpillars** eat leaves.
Tense	In English, to show past, present and future tense shifts, the verb changes. This often involves adding a word to show this. Some verbs behave irregularly from the standard rules. Here are three basic tenses; more can be found in a grammar book or language learner's dictionary.	*Simple Present Future* *past* I studied study shall study You studied study will study S/he studied studies will study We studied study shall study You studied study will study They studied study will study
Verb	The action or 'doing' word in a sentence. It changes form to indicate shifts in time (see tense).	I work, I am working, I will work, I worked, I was working, I have worked, I had worked.

Table 12.3 Twelve common grammar errors

Problem area	Incorrect example (✗) and correction (✓)
1 Comparing Sometimes there is confusion with when to use a word ending in -er or -est rather than using 'more' or 'most'. For grammar book entries, look for **Comparatives** and **Superlatives**.	Comparing two things: ✗ The debit was more bigger than the credit. ✓ The debit was grea**ter** than the credit. Comparing three or more things: ✗ China has the most greatest population in the world. ✓ China has the grea**test** population in the world. Countable and non-countable: ✗ There were less cases of meningitis last year. ✓ There were fewer cases of meningitis last year. (Countable) ✗ There was fewer snow last year. ✓ There was less snow last year. (Non-countable)
2 Describing Commas can be vital to meaning – misuse can cause fundamental changes to meaning. For grammar book entry, look for **Relative clauses**.	✗ Toys, which are dangerous, should not be given to children. (Inference: all toys are dangerous – not what the author means) ✓ Toys which are dangerous should not be given to children. (Inference: only safe toys should be given to children – what the author means)
3 Encapsulating Using one word to represent a previous word or idea. For grammar book entry, look for **Demonstrative pronoun**.	✗ ... impact of diesel use on air quality. **This** increases in rush-hour. (Inference: air quality increases in rush hour – not the intended meaning.) ✓ ... impact of diesel use on air quality. **This impact** increases in rush-hour.
4 Its/it's These two are often confused. For grammar book entry, look for **Possessives (its)** and **Apostrophes (it's)**.	✗ As it's aim, the book describes the whole problem. ✓ As its aim, the book describes the whole problem. (Possession) ✗ Its not a viable answer to the problem. ✓ It's not a viable answer to the problem (It is ...) ✗ Its not had a good review. ✓ It's not had a good review. (It has ...)
5 Joining Words such as 'because', 'but' and 'and' join two clauses; they should never begin sentences. For grammar book entry, look for **Conjunctions**.	✗ Because the sample was too small, the results were invalid. ✓ Since the sample was too small, the results were invalid. ('Because' is a conjunction and is used to join two ideas.) ✗ But the UN failed to act. And the member states did nothing. ✓ The country was attacked, **but** the UN failed to act **and** the member states did nothing. ('But' and 'and' are conjunctions that join two separate ideas.)

Table 12.3 continued

Problem area	Incorrect example (✗) and correction (✓)
6 Double negative Two negatives mean a positive. Sometimes using a double negative can cause confusion. For grammar book entry, look for **Double negatives**.	✗ They have not had no results from their experiments. ✓ They have not had any results from their experiments. ✗ The government had not done nothing to alleviate poverty. ✓ The government had done nothing to alleviate poverty. (Intended meaning.)
7 Past participles These are sometimes misused, especially when the verbs are irregular in past forms. For grammar book entry, look for **Past participles**.	✗ The team had **went** to present their findings at the conference. ✓ The team had **gone** to present their findings at the conference.
8 Prepositions These should not come at the end of a sentence. For grammar book entry, look for **Prepositions**.	✗ These figures are the ones you will work with. ✓ These figures are the ones with which you will work.
9 Pronouns These are used to replace nouns. The singular pronouns often cause confusion because they need to agree with the verb. For grammar book entry, look for **Pronouns**.	**Singular pronouns:** anybody, anyone, anything, each, either, everybody, everyone, everything, neither, nobody, no one, nothing, somebody, someone, something – all take a singular verb. ✗ Each of the new measures are to be introduced separately. ✓ **Each** of the new measures **is** to be introduced separately. **Reflexive pronouns:** ✗ Although disappointed, they only have theirselves to blame. ✓ Although disappointed, **they** only have **themselves** to blame.
10 Specifying Words that are used to identify specific singular and plural items must match. For grammar book entry, look for **Demonstratives**.	✓ **This** kind of mistake **is** common. ✓ **These** kinds of mistakes **are** less common. ✓ **That** result **is** acceptable. ✓ **Those** results **are** not acceptable.

Table 12.3 continued

Problem area	Incorrect example (✗) and correction (✓)
11 Subject–verb agreement Often singular subjects are matched with plural verbs and vice versa. For grammar book entry, look for **Subject–verb agreement**.	✗ The Principal, together with the Chancellor, were present. ✓ The Principal, together with the Chancellor, was present. ✗ It is the result of these overtures and influences that help to mould personal identity. ✓ It is the **result** of these overtures and influences that **helps** to mould personal identity.
12 There/their/they're These simply need to be remembered. For grammar book entry, look for **Words that are often confused**.	✗ They finished there work before noon. ✓ They finished **their** work before noon. ✗ We have six places at the conference. We'll go their. ✓ We have six places at the conference. We'll go **there**. ✗ Researchers are skilled but there not highly paid. ✓ Researchers are skilled but **they're** not highly paid.

→ How to use grammar checkers to best advantage

Some software packages provide a grammar-checking facility. Although this can provide you with some helpful tips, it is important to recognise that it is not infallible. As an artificial intelligence device, it cannot always fully respond to more sophisticated grammatical logic. For example, in the following sentence, the words 'a lot of' were underlined as grammatically incorrect by an electronic grammar checker:

You get <u>a lot of</u> help for projects from the tutors.

The suggested adjustment was to rewrite the sentence as:

You get <u>many</u> help for projects from the tutors.

This is obviously grammatically incorrect. In another example using the passive voice:

The limitation of feedback from teaching staff was noted by other students to be frustrating.

was 'corrected' to:

Other students to be frustrating noted the limitation of feedback from teaching staff.

This clearly makes nonsense of the original text and meaning. The message is clear: you should not blindly accept all changes recommended by the grammar checker.

If you have had an error pointed out to you, but don't understand it fully, then ask the person who made the correction to explain to you what is wrong. If you are unable to do this or are unsure, then check out some of the resources given below. You can do a little bit of detective work first by looking at your error in conjunction with the grammar definition list in Table 12.2. Once you have an idea of what the problem might be, then you could consult one of the many good grammar books available by looking for the key grammatical term in the index or contents. For example, you could have a look at *Longman's Advanced Learners' Grammar* (Foley and Hall, 2003), which has very useful diagnostic tests to help you identify difficulties. The book gives clear explanations of each grammar point with exercises for practice and an answer key. Another source is *Fowler's Modern English Usage* (Fowler and Winchester, 2002). Other user-friendly sources include the *BBC English Dictionary* (1992) or the *Longman Dictionary of Contemporary English* (2003), both of which give words, meanings and examples of correct usage.

Practical tips for understanding grammar

Identify and understand your errors. Markers of your assignments often indicate errors on written work, sometimes simply by underlining or circling text, sometimes by restructuring or inserting a correction. It is well worth spending some time looking over your marked work to understand different points that the marker has identified – some will be related to subject matter, some to grammar and some to punctuation. If you can isolate the latter two types, noting the errors and how these have been corrected, then you are well on the way to avoiding them in the future. This could make a real difference to you in your marks on future assignments.

Make your own checklist. Once you have identified an error that you have made, then make a note of it (you could keep a glossary notebook and isolate a few pages for grammar points). It's a good idea to write down the error, its correction and, if you can, a quick note of what is wrong and why.

12.1 Get into the habit of consulting reference works when required. The grammar of most languages can be complex, but if you approach it on a 'need-to-know' basis, then you could make a point of learning those things that are most relevant to your need. For example, some students find it difficult to work out when to use a particular tense, so they could look up that section in a grammar book and find out what they need. Other students might have difficulty with working out how the passive operates; again, they could look up that section in a grammar book to find out more.

12.2 Set up a section in a notebook for keeping a record of errors that have arisen in your writing. Note the error, its correction and also a reference to a source where you were able to find some information on the particular grammar point. The act of writing these details down will help you to memorise the grammar rule – but if you don't, the notebook will act as a useful personal reference.

12.3 Try to learn more grammar with the help of others. It's said that some people have a greater aptitude for understanding language – it's a kind of code, after all, and if no one has ever given you the key then it is not surprising if you cannot 'break the code'. If this is the case for you, and someone has made a comment about your written grammar, then ask friends if they know what is wrong with the word, sentence or paragraph. They may have some more knowledge of the grammar codes and be able to help by explaining to you what is wrong.

Better punctuation

How to use punctuation marks appropriately

Punctuation is an important 'code' that helps the reader understand your message. If you misuse it, ignore it or abuse it, you will not be transmitting your ideas clearly and, indeed, may confuse your reader. This chapter lays out some of the principles of standard punctuation and gives you some tips on how to avoid punctuation errors.

Key topics:
→ Why punctuation is important
→ Punctuation guidelines

Key terms
Ambiguous   Capital letter   Genre   Inverted commas   Parenthesis
Proper noun

Consider how people speak – they use gestures, intonation and pauses to indicate emphasis, astonishment, suspense and a whole range of other emotions and ideas. In writing, punctuation helps to send these signals by splitting up or joining ideas – for example, by using the full-stop (.), exclamation mark (!), question mark (?), comma (,), colon (:), and semicolon (;).

Similarly, other signals are used to inform the reader of ideas that may not be those of the writer – for example, quotation marks ('...') to indicate what someone else said or wrote; or apostrophes (') to explain the idea of ownership (for example, 'the student's bursary').

→ Why punctuation is important

Punctuation is essential and has evolved as an aid to the reader to help convey meaning, emphasis and style. It is a recognised code and learning how to use that code contributes to your skill as a writer.

Table 13.1 Simplified rules of punctuation

Punctuation	Mark	How the mark is used
Apostrophe	. . .'	• For possession: e.g. Napoleon's armies (singular owner); students' essays (plural owner) • For contraction: e.g. Don't cry; I'm hungry; it's late • But note: As **its** central theme, the book considered wind power (no apostrophe required at **its** – possessive of 'it')
Brackets (parenthesis)	[. . .] (. . .)	• Square brackets [. . .]: for adding your own words within a quote • Round brackets (. . .): to isolate explanatory information
Capital letter	ABC etc.	• Starts sentences, proper nouns, seasons, rivers, mountain ranges, places, Acts of Parliament, titles, organisations
Colon	:	• Leads from one clause to another: e.g. from introduction to main point, from statement to example, from cause to effect • Introduces lists (examples throughout this book) • Introduces a 'long quote'
Comma	,	• Separates items in a list of three or more: e.g. tea, beer, juice and wine • Separates part of a sentence: e.g. He came home, ate and fell asleep • Separates additional information within a sentence: e.g. Rugby, in the main, is a contact sport • Marks adverbs: e.g. Certainly, the results have been positive
Dash	–	• Marks an aside/addition: e.g. Murder – regardless of the reason – is a crime
Ellipsis	. . .	• Marks words omitted from a quotation: e.g. 'taxes . . . mean price rises'
Exclamation mark	!	• Shows shock, horror (rarely used in academic writing): e.g. Help!

If you look back at a piece of your own work, you will probably be more aware of your own punctuation 'style'. This will probably involve using particular sentence structures repeatedly and favouring certain punctuation marks over others. If you want to add variety to your writing, you can do this by consciously trying to use a variety of forms of punctuation, and thereby changing the structure of some of your sentences. Simplified rules for punctuation marks are provided in Table 13.1.

Table 13.1 continued

Punctuation	Mark	How the mark is used
Full stop	.	• Marks the end of a sentence: e.g. This is the end. • Marks an abbreviation where the last letter of the abbreviation is *not* the last letter of the complete word: e.g. Prof. etc., i.e., m.p.h., p.a.
Hyphen	–	• Joins a single letter to an existing word: e.g. x-ray • Separates prefixes: e.g. post-modern • Prevents repetition of certain letters: e.g. semi-independent • Joins a prefix to a proper noun: e.g. pro-British • Creates a noun from a phrasal verb: e.g. show-off • Joins numbers and fractions: e.g. twenty-three; three-quarters • Indicates a compound modifier where two adjectives or noun adjectives are used to describe something: e.g., orange-red skirt.
Italics	*italics*	• Differentiates text to show quotations, titles of publications in citations, species, works of art, foreign words: e.g. *déjà vu*; *et al.*
Question mark	?	• Ends sentences that ask a direct question: e.g. Who am I?
Quotation marks (inverted commas)	'. . .' ". . ."	• 'Single quotation marks' mark exact words spoken/printed in a text, or 'special' words • "Double quotation marks" place a quotation within a quotation (British English) • Note that in some word-processing packages it is possible to choose between 'smart quotes' (". . .") and 'straight quotes' (". . .")
Semicolon	;	• Separates two or more clauses of equal importance: e.g. They won the battle; the other side won the war • Separates listed items, especially when description uses several words

Sometimes punctuation is essential in order to convey the meaning intended, otherwise a sentence can be ambiguous – that is, have more than one meaning. For example:

1 The inspector said the teacher is a fool.

2 'The inspector', said the teacher, 'is a fool'.

3 The inspector said, 'The teacher is a fool'.

These three sentences show that punctuation makes a critical difference to meaning. The first one *reports* what the inspector said; the second is *what the teacher actually said* about the inspector being a fool; the third is *what the inspector actually said* about the teacher being a fool.

Where punctuation is omitted entirely, then it is difficult to identify separate points. For example:

> The character of james bond created by ian fleming portrayed a fastliving but urbane spy whose coolness was apparently imperturbable he became a real screen hero.

Without punctuation, this text becomes simply a string of words rather than a meaningful set of statements. (The correct version is on p. 134.)

→ Punctuation guidelines

In some respects, the way that punctuation rules are applied depends on the conventions of different genres, that is, the categories of writing. In fiction, for example, the rules are followed less rigidly, and sometimes do not follow the rules exactly as they would in a non-fiction book, such as an academic text.

For your purposes as a student, it is important that you follow the punctuation codes correctly as this will reflect on how others judge the quality of your work. In some disciplines, marks may be deducted for punctuation errors. Table 13.2 gives examples of the more common errors.

---

smart tip

Overuse of certain punctuation marks

Two punctuation marks that are commonly overused in students' academic writing are parentheses and exclamation marks.

- Parentheses are sometimes a symptom of 'lazy' writing (or a feeling that you need to add more detail than you probably require). If you feel you have a tendency to use parentheses excessively, you can often replace these marks with commas.

- It is rare that an exclamation mark is appropriate in academic writing! This can be seen in the example of the previous sentence, where the exclamation mark is essentially unnecessary. If you find you use exclamation marks a lot, these can often be simply replaced with a full stop with no great loss of effect.

Sentences

These begin with capital letters and finish with either a full stop, a question mark or an exclamation mark. In a sentence that ends with a quote, the full stop comes after the final quote mark 'like this'. If, however, the quotation looks as though it is probably a complete sentence, or if more than one sentence is quoted, then the full stop precedes the final quote mark. (Similarly, a complete sentence within parentheses has the full stop inside the final bracket, as in this sentence.)

'Open' and 'closed' punctuation

'Open' in this context means using minimal punctuation. While this has gained some acceptance in letter-writing, it is not universally accepted within the academic world.

- *Example of open punctuation:*

  Dr Douglas M Kay the world famous projectile designer outlined his research at the conference in St Albans for staff of the Ministry of Defence (MOD) and the Foreign Office (FO).

- *Example of closed punctuation:*

  Dr. Douglas M. Kay, the world-famous projectile designer, outlined his research at the conference in St. Albans for staff of the Ministry of Defence (M.O.D.) and the Foreign Office (F.O.).

Note that full stops are not generally used if the last letter of a contraction is also the last letter of the full word (Mr, Dr) or in abbreviations such as TV or in acronyms such as BBC, NATO, UNICEF, scuba, and so on.

You may come across both these styles of punctuation in your reading. This disparity often arises from transatlantic differences in punctuation styles. However, since academic writing is often complex in its structure, generally the academic world tends to favour the more traditional 'closed' punctuation style.

Paragraph alignment

Although not strictly punctuation, this can greatly affect layout and readability of text. Paragraphs can be aligned in two ways: fully justified (blocked) and indented (see pp. 118 and 213).

Table 13.2 Common punctuation errors and their corrections. The following common errors with their corrections should help you to find an answer to most punctuation dilemmas.

Punctuation mark	Error	Correction	Explanation
1.1 Apostrophes: singular	The **Principals'** Committee will meet at noon today.	Principal's	There is only one Principal, therefore the apostrophe goes immediately after the word 'Principal'. Then add the s to make it correctly possessive.
1.2 Apostrophes: plural	The **womens'** team beat the mens' team by 15 points and the **childrens'** team beat them both. The **boy's** team won the prize.	women's men's children's boys'	The words 'women', 'men' and 'children' are plural words. To make them possessive, just add an apostrophe after the plural word and add 's'. The word 'boys' is a plural and is a regularly formed plural, thus, the apostrophe comes after the 's'.
1.3 Apostrophes: contractions	**Its** not a good time to sell a property. **Its** been up for sale for ages. **Well** need to lower the price.	It's = it is It's = it has We'll = we shall	'It's' is a contracted form of the words 'it is' or 'it has'. In this case, the sentence means: 'It is not a good time to sell a property'.
1.4 Apostrophes: not needed	The **tomatoes'** cost 60 pence a kilo.	tomatoes	The word 'tomatoes' is a plural. No apostrophe is needed to make words plural.
1.5 Apostrophes: not needed	The Charter includes human rights in **it's** terms.	its	No apostrophe needed to show possession. 'Its' is the exception to the general rule of adding apostrophes to indicate possession. You will see the potential conflict with the contraction for 'it is', above (see also p. 130).
2.1 Capital letters: sentences	**the** first day of the term is tomorrow.	The	The first letter of the first word of a sentence in English always needs a capital letter.
2.2 Capital letters: proper names	The **prime minister** is the first **lord** of the **treasury**. The **north atlantic treaty organisation** is a regional organisation. Pearls found in the **river tay** are of considerable value.	Prime Minister; First Lord of the Treasury North Atlantic Treaty Organisation River Tay	Proper nouns for roles, names of organisations, rivers, mountains, lochs, lakes and place names. These all require a capital for all parts of the name.

3 Colon	A number of aspects will be covered, **including** ● Energy conservation ● Pollution limitation ● Cost control	... including: ● energy conservation; ● pollution limitation; ● cost control.	A colon to introduce the list. Each item, except the last one, should be finished with a semicolon. No capital is necessary at each bullet if the list follows from an incomplete sentence introducing the list.
4.1 Commas	**The leader of the group Dr Joan Jones** was not available for comment.	The leader of the group, Dr Joan Jones, was not available for comment.	This is a common error. The name of the person gives more information about the leader; thus, the person's name needs to be inserted with commas before and after.
4.2 Commas	There are several member-states that do not support this view. They are **Britain France Germany Portugal and Greece.**	There are several member-states that do not support this view. They are Britain, France, Germany, Portugal, and Greece.	Strictly speaking, when making a list such as in the example, a comma should come before 'and'. This is called the 'Oxford comma' and its use has caused much debate. However, increasingly, the comma is being omitted before the word 'and' in lists such as this one.
4.3 Commas	**However** we have no evidence to support this statement.	However, we have no evidence to support this statement.	The 'signposting' words often used at the beginning of sentences are followed by a comma. Some of the more common of these words are: hence, however, in addition, moreover, nevertheless, therefore, thus.
4.4 Commas	**Although we have had significant rainfall** the reservoirs are low.	Although we have had significant rainfall, the reservoirs are low.	When a sentence begins with 'although', then the sentence has two parts. The part that gives the idea of concession in this sentence is 'Although we have had significant rainfall'. The second part gives us the impact of that concession, in this case, that 'the reservoirs are low'. A comma is used to divide these parts.
4.5 Commas	**To demonstrate competence** it is important to be able to face challenges.	To demonstrate competence, it is important to be able to face challenges.	Another way to write this sentence would be: 'It is important to be able to face challenges to demonstrate competence'. By putting the phrase 'to demonstrate competence' at the beginning of the sentence, it places emphasis on the idea of competence and, in order to make that word-order distinction, a comma is needed.
5 Ellipsis	There is a deficit in the budget ...... brought on by mismanagement at the highest level.	There is a deficit in the budget ... brought on by mismanagement at the highest level.	Ellipsis marks always consist of three dots, no more. These are used to show that some words from the original statement have been omitted (see also p. 193).

Punctuation of bulleted and numbered lists

Minimal punctuation

The causes of migration include:

- drought
- famine
- disease.

Famine relief agencies:

1 UN
2 OXFAM
3 Save the Children.

The list as a sentence

Population decreases because:

- drought dries up pastures;
- people do not have food;
- lack of food lowers resistance to disease; or
- people either die or migrate.

To save your document:

1 click on File;
2 select Save As;
3 choose directory;
4 choose file name; and
5 click on Save.

Note that the use of lists in text is not favoured in some disciplines.

If in doubt about punctuation, the guiding principle should be whether the addition of a punctuation symbol adds to the clarity.

Lists

These can be compiled using a variety of bullet-point or numerical styles. Use numbered lists when there is an inherent priority, hierarchy or sequence. Where the list is preceded by the beginning of a sentence, you should introduce the list with a colon (:). The follow-on words in the list should begin with lower-case letters and each item, except the last one, should be finished with a semicolon. By some conventions, list items have capitalised initials, while 'and' is optional after the colon for the second-last item on the lists. The final point finishes with a full stop.

Practical tips for clear punctuation

Checking your punctuation is appropriate. Read your work aloud at a reasonable pace - imagine that you are a television newsreader who has to convey the item so that it makes sense. As you read, your ear will identify the pauses and inconsistencies in your text in a way that sometimes the most careful silent editing misses. For example, if you need to pause for breath, there is a chance that you need to insert a comma or start a new sentence.

Using symbols to help proof-read your work. It is helpful to print out a hard copy of your draft text and then to go through it methodically, marking it with the proof-reading symbols (**Ch 16**) in both the text and the margin. This will help you to go through your work systematically on-screen at a later point. The double-entry method helps to ensure that you don't miss out any of your corrections.

Using lists, bullet points and sub-headings. In some disciplines it is permissible to use sub-headings and bulleted or numbered lists. This strategy enables you to avoid some of the pitfalls of punctuation, but it is not universally accepted in academic writing. If you do use devices such as bullets and lists, then you need to observe the punctuation conventions shown opposite. Some people use sub-headings to help them focus on writing content and then, when finished writing, they replace the sub-headings with a topic sentence.

(GO) And now . . .

13.1 Use punctuation to avoid ambiguity. Go back to the example about James Bond and insert punctuation so that the meaning of the text is clear. The correct version should read:

The character of James Bond, created by Ian Fleming, portrayed a fast-living but urbane spy, whose coolness was apparently imperturbable. He became a real screen hero.

13.2 Follow textbooks as good models of punctuation. Go to a textbook in your own subject area and find some text that shows use of some of the less frequently used punctuation marks, for example, colons, semicolons, italics, square brackets, round brackets and apostrophes. Consider how these have been used and how the textbook usage conforms to the punctuation style described in Table 13.1 and Table 13.2.

13.3 If you feel your knowledge of punctuation is poor, pick up a specialist guide. There are a number of good punctuation guides available in libraries and bookshops, such as the *Penguin Guide to Punctuation* (Trask, 2004). Have a browse through some of these and identify one that you find particularly user-friendly. Consider this as a purchase that will provide you with a ready reference for years.

Better spelling

How to spell competently

Spellcheckers make life easy, but doing the checking takes time and you won't always have access to a spellchecking facility, as when using a word processor. This chapter looks at some of the basic rules of spelling and gives some examples of these rules. It also looks at 'irregular' words that are often used in academic contexts and also at some words that are commonly misspelt.

Key topics:
→ Words to watch
→ Using spellcheckers
→ Spelling dictionaries

Key terms
Adjective   Adverb   Consonant   Noun   Prefix   Suffix   Syllable
Typo   Vowel

Some people will have been routinely taught to spell at school, others may not. Whichever category applies to you, developing your spelling skill is an ongoing process. This chapter explains the basic spelling rules and gives examples of how they work. If you are unfamiliar with some of the words, then you might find it useful to check these out before you begin (see Table 14.1).

→ Words to watch

English is a language that has borrowed quite freely from other languages and this means that many of the spelling 'rules' are quite diverse. For many words, where there is a 'rule' more often than not there are exceptions to that rule. This means that you simply need to learn these exceptions.

Table 14.1 **Twenty basic spelling rules.** In English the 'rules' are difficult to define because frequently there are exceptions to them. Here are some of the fundamental rules, with some examples of exceptions where these occur.

Rule		Examples, with exceptions as applicable
1	i comes before e (except after c)	belief, chief relief, science, sufficient *but* receive, perceive, deceive, ceiling seize, vein, weird, leisure
2	**Verbs:** where verbs end in -eed and -ede, then the -eed ending goes with suc-/ex-/pro-; -ede applies in all other cases	-eed: succ**eed**, exc**eed**, proc**eed** -ede: prec**ede**, conc**ede**
3	**Verbs:** where verbs end with -ise, nouns end with -ice	practise (verb)/practice (noun) *but* exercise: verb and noun
4	**Double** final consonants before using -ing when the words are single syllable and end with b/d/g/m/n/p/r/t	robbing, ridding, bagging, summing, running, hopper, furred, fittest
	Double consonant when the stressed syllable is at the end of the word	occurred, beginning, forgettable
	Double l when words end in an l preceded by a short vowel	travelled, levelled
5	**Nouns** ending in -our drop the u in the adjective form	glamour/glamorous, humour/humorous
6	**Plurals** generally add -s, or -es after -ss/x/ch/sh/	boys, cats, dogs; crosses, fixes, churches, dishes
	Nouns ending in -y drop -y and add -ies	ally/allies, copy/copies *but* monkeys, donkeys
	Nouns ending in -o add -s for the plural	photos, pianos *but* tomatoes, volcanoes, heroes
	Nouns ending in -f and -fe: no consistent rule	Chief/chiefs *but* half/halves
	Some 'foreign' nouns follow the rules of their own language	medium/media, criterion/criteria, datum/data, bureau/bureaux
	Hyphenated words	brothers-in-law, commanders-in-chief (not brother-in-laws/commander-in-chiefs)
	Some nouns are the same format for singular and for plural	sheep, fish
7	**Prefixes** dis- and mis- plus noun or verb (no double 's'); but where such words begin with an 's', insert prefix (do not drop 's')	dis + agree, mis + manage, *note* dis + satisfaction, mis + spell

▶

Table 14.1 continued

Rule		Examples, with exceptions as applicable
8	**Suffixes** -ful, -fully, -al, -ally: adjectives formed with the suffix -ful and -al have only one l	careful, hopeful *but* carefully, hopefully
	When forming adverbs, add -ly	skilfully, marginally
	Adjectives ending in -ic form their adverbs with -ally	basic/basically
9	**Compound words**: where there is a 'double l' in one of the words, one l may be dropped	Well + fare = welfare; un + till = until *but* well + being = wellbeing; ill + ness = illness
10	**Silent** e: usually keep -e when adding the suffix	hope + full = hopeful
	If suffix begins with a vowel, then drop final -e	come + ing = coming
	After words ending in -ce or -ge, keep -e to keep sounds soft when suffix is added	noticeable, courageous
11	For words ending in -y that are preceded by a consonant, change -y to -i before any suffix except -ing, -ist, -ish	dry/driest *but* drying, copyist, dryish cronyism
12	For words ending in -ic or -ac, add -k before -ing, -ed or -er	trafficking, mimic/mimicked, picnic/picnicker
13	For 'joins' within word, do not add or subtract letters at 'join'	meanness
14	**Silent** letters. In certain cases, the letters b, g, k, l, p and w are silent	debt, gnat, knot, palm, psychiatrist, wrong
15	**Latin** words in English ending in -ix or -ex in the singular, end in -ices in the plural	appendix/appendices, index/indices
16	**Latin** words in English ending in -um in the singular, generally end in -a i the plural	datum/data, medium/media, stratum/strata
17	**Latin** words in English ending in -us in the singular, generally end in -i in the plural	radius/radii
18	**Latin** words in English ending in -a in the singular, end in -ae in the plural	agenda/agendae, formula/formulae
19	**Greek** words in English ending in -ion in the singular, end in -ia in the plural	criterion/criteria
20	**Greek** words in English ending in -sis in the singular, end in -ses in the plural	analysis/analyses, hypothesis/hypotheses

Table 14.2 provides a listing of words that are often misspelt in academic written work. In addition, some words are often confused with words that are either similar in meaning or have a similar 'word shape', and so people often transpose letters in the middle of a word: for example, 'goal' and 'gaol'. Both words are correctly spelt, but they are different in meaning. Some of the most commonly confused 'pairs' are given in Table 14.3.

Table 14.2 **Some words that are often misspelt in academic work**

Correct spelling examples	Incorrect spelling examples
argument	arguement
believe	beleive
Britain	Britian
bulletin	buletin
campaign	campane
committee	comitee
commitment	comitment
embarrass	embaras
February	Febuary
government	goverment
immediate	imediate
jeopardy	jepardy
maintenance	maintainance
necessary	neccessary
parliament	parlament
privilege	priviledge
receive	recieve
separate	seperate
Wednesday	Wedensday
weather	wether
whether	wether

Table 14.3 Some word pairs that are commonly confused. The sense is given in parentheses. These pairs are similar in pronunciation. This can cause confusion and means that they are more likely to the written incorrectly.

accent (speech)	ascent (climb)
aerial (antenna)	arial (font)
affect (change - verb)	effect (change - noun)
aisle (passage)	isle (small island)
aloud (audible)	allowed (permitted)
ascend (climb - verb)	ascent (climb - noun)
bare (uncovered)	bear (animal/to carry)
blew (past form: blow)	blue (colour)
board (strip of timber)	bored (wearied of)
born (birth)	borne (endure)
canvas (strong fabric)	canvass (get opinion)
cereal (grain)	serial (in a row)
choose (present form: select)	chose (past form: select)
complement (enhance)	compliment (praise)
constituency (electoral area)	consistency (texture of liquid)
council (committee)	counsel (advice/adviser)
currant (dried grape)	current (present/flow)
desert (sand, or abandon)	dessert (pudding)
discreet (tactful)	discrete (stand-alone)
draft (first copy)	draught (wind)
forward (toward front)	foreword (book preface)
heal (to make whole)	heel (part of foot)
hear (to listen)	here (at this place)
holy (sacred)	wholly (completely)
loan (money)	lone (single)
lose (misplace)	loose (slack)
lose (misplace - verb)	loss (item lost - noun)
mail (post)	male (gender)
peace (tranquillity)	piece (portion)
plaice (fish)	place (location)
plain (ordinary)	plane (tree/aircraft)
practice (noun)	practise (verb)
principal (main idea/person)	principle (fundamental)

Table 14.3 continued

root (part of plant)	**route** (journey)
scene (part of a play)	**seen** (past form: saw)
seize (grab)	**cease** (stop)
sight (sense of seeing)	**site** (location)
stationary (not moving)	**stationery** (pens, writing material)
weather (climate)	**whether** (as alternative)
were (past tense: are)	**where** (place)

→ Using spellcheckers

The commonly used word-processing packages have a spellchecking facility. This will alert you to possible misspellings by underlining a word that the package does not recognise. That allows you to go back and check the word in a standard dictionary if the error is not a simple 'typo'. Some systems will allow you to add words to the package dictionary so that a common error will automatically be changed as you mistype it. In Word, this facility is found under Tools/Autocorrect. You can usually add words of your own choice to the dictionary part of the software package, for instance, the technical jargon for your discipline.

However, despite all these aids, you should still be very conscientious about proof-reading your work. The spellchecker will accept any word that is in its dictionary so that, for example, if you type 'bear wires', the spellchecker will accept this as both words are correctly spelt, although what you really meant was 'bare wires' (see Table 14.3). At the same time, the word-processing dictionary will not always have a word that you are looking for. In that case, you will need to check the spelling in a dictionary – off the shelf or online (**Ch 5**).

→ Spelling dictionaries

If you find that spelling is a particular difficulty for you, then consider buying a spelling dictionary. Some of these dictionaries not only give the correct spelling but also list typical misspelt formats with the correct format alongside. **Ch 15** gives some further information about spelling and other types of dictionary.

Practical tips for spelling accurately

Avoid using alternatives to standard spelling. For example, it is not advisable to use text-messaging language because examination scripts have to be written in standard English. In any case, the fact that the marker may not be as 'fluent' in the use of text-speak could mean that your point may not be understood.

Learn the correct spelling of the key words in your discipline. Specialist terms need to be accurately spelt. For example, if you are studying politics, then it is advisable to learn how to spell 'parliament' correctly. Likewise, if you are studying a scientific subject, then it is important to know that the plural of 'formula' is 'formulae' and that 'data' is a plural word with a singular 'datum'. In some disciplines American English is used as the international standard: for example, in chemistry 'sulfur' is used rather than the British English 'sulphur'.

Check on the correct form of a word. If you look up the root form of the word in a good dictionary (which probably means a big dictionary), then you will find the different forms of the word, including its plural, if it is deviant from the rules in any way, will be shown under the headword (see Figure 15.1). It's worth checking this out because the very act of looking the word up in the dictionary will help to seal it in your memory.

GO And now . . .

14.1 Create a glossary-style memory sheet. You may wish to model this on the one suggested in Table 15.4. Add the correct spelling of key words that you know you frequently get wrong. This will help you remember them and also give you a ready reference to double-check while you are writing.

14.2 Test yourself from the words in Table 14.3. Ask someone to read out these words and meanings. You can then test yourself to establish how many of them you can spell correctly. Add any that you consistently get wrong to your glossary memory sheet.

14.3 If you are having difficulty with spelling, then look for a spelling dictionary in your university or public library. Look up some words that you frequently misspell and assess whether this kind of dictionary would be a help to you. If you think it would, then you might consider buying one for yourself.

How to increase your word-power

Whatever your discipline, you will find that, as a university student, you increasingly meet new words. These can be terms that are special to your subject as well as words that are used to explain and discuss topics within your study areas. This chapter suggests some strategies to help you expand your vocabulary gradually, so that you can develop your powers of expression in your written work.

Key topics:

→ Glossaries
→ Standard dictionaries
→ Using a thesaurus
→ Specialist dictionaries

Key terms
Antonym Glossary Headword Phonetic Prefix Suffix Synonym

Expanding your vocabulary is something that you will find is essential, particularly as you start out on your studies. Many disciplines have their own terminology, sometimes called jargon, and you may need to master this before understanding higher-level concepts. Also, the expectation in academic writing is that you use words effectively and correctly, and this implies having a wide vocabulary and expressions to use in the appropriate contexts.

→ Glossaries

Textbooks in many subject areas now provide fairly comprehensive glossaries at the beginning or end of the book to help the reader to confirm the meaning of a term quickly. Sometimes textbooks provide a list of key words at the beginning of each chapter to identify new or specialist use of terminology.

All this is useful to you as you read, but you may find it helpful to create your own glossary that it is tailor-made to your personal needs. Access to a good dictionary will be essential to help you build this up, to check on precise meanings, and to help you avoid using slang expressions or words that are too informal.

---

smart tip

Three ways to expand your vocabulary

1 Use a dictionary to check on the meaning of new words you come across.

2 Use a thesaurus to find new words of similar meaning (synonyms) to ones you already know. If unsure, you should check words found in a thesaurus for their *precise* meaning, as this may differ subtly from what you intend.

3 Maintain a glossary of jargon terms and meanings of words unfamiliar to you.

→ Standard dictionaries

Dictionaries vary in size and complexity. For example, some give words, pronunciation and meanings, while others also give examples of correct usage. Your university library will hold a number of different types of dictionary in the reference section and may also provide access to an online dictionary as part of its e-resource bank.

Figure 15.1 shows a typical dictionary entry. From this entry you will be able to identify the form of the word as it is used in your text, or, if you are writing, it will help you choose the correct form for your own work. Each entry is introduced by a headword and this is followed by information about its different forms, for example noun, verb, adjective, and so on. Terms are explained in Figure 15.2 and Tables 15.1 and 15.2. Table 15.3 describes some features of dictionaries and thesauri that can be accessed in hard copy and electronically.

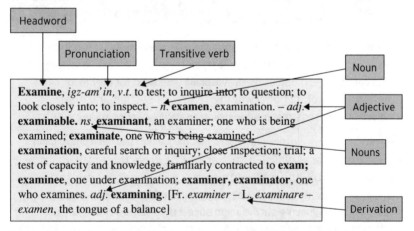

Figure 15.1 A standard dictionary entry, showing different parts and abbreviations.

Source: The Chambers Dictionary, 2003. Edinburgh: Chambers Harrap Publishers Ltd.

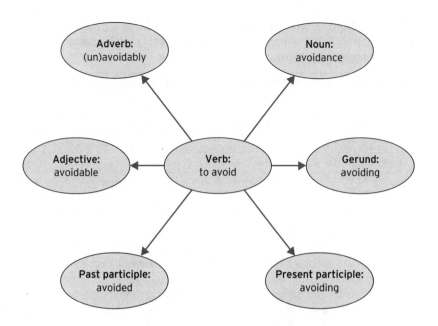

Examples of how to use these types of words in sentences:

Verb	Countries **avoid** war at all costs.
Noun	The **avoidance** of war is a primary objective of diplomats.
Gerund	**Avoiding** conscription in time of war is something many people strive to do.
Present participle	Students are **avoiding** the exams by trying to obtain exemptions.
Past participle	Students have **avoided** the topics that they found most difficult.
Adjective	War is **avoidable** when diplomacy is successful.
Adverb	The judge stated that the plaintiff had been **unavoidably** delayed.

Figure 15.2 Word families. As you expand your vocabulary you will find that you know the word you want to use, but it may not look or sound quite 'right' in your text. This may be because you have not used the word in its correct form. This diagram explains some of the key grammatical terms with examples. Table 15.1 shows some of the more common word beginnings (prefixes) and Table 15.2 shows endings (suffixes) that identify the different forms of words in English.

Table 15.1 Prefixes: word beginnings. This table shows how, by adding a letter or letters at the beginning of a word, the meaning can be changed. These beginnings are called prefixes.

Prefix	Meaning	Example
a–	on	aboard
a–, ab–, abs–	away from	avert, abuse, abstain
ad–, ac–, ar–	to	adventure, access, arrange
ante–	before	antenatal
anti–	against	antihistamine
bi–	two	biped
circum–	around	circumscribe, circumnavigate
com–, con–	together	communicate, convene
contra–	against	contrast
de–	down	depose
dif–, dis–	apart, not	differ, discredit
ex–	out of	exit
fore–	before	foreknowledge
il–	not	illegible
im–, in–	in, into	implode, intrude
im–, in–	not	immature, inescapable
inter–	between	interact
ir–	not	irregular
mis–	wrong	misplace
ob–	against	obscure
post–	after	post-modern
pre–	before	prerequisite
pro–	forth	progress
re–	back	regress
sub–	under	subtract
trans–	across	transmit
un–	not	unpopular
vice–	instead	vice-president

Table 15.2(a) Suffixes: word endings. This table shows the endings (suffixes) that can be added to the root verb to change the form of the word. Thus, taking the example in Figure 15.2, the root verb is 'avoid' and, to make the noun, the noun ending '-ance' is added. To make the adjective, add '-able'.

Verbs	Nouns			Adjectives		Adverbs
-ain	-aint	-ing	-able	-ic	-ly
-ave	-al	-iour	-al	-ing	
-el	-ance	-ment	-ar	-ious	
-en	-cy	-ness	-ate	-ish	
-ify	-dom	-sion	-ent	-ite	
-ise	-ence	-son	-eous	-ive	
-ive	-ery	-th	-esque	-less	
-ise	-ice	-tion	-ful	-ous	
-uce	-ief	-y	-ial		

Table 15.2(b) Suffix meanings. Some suffixes have particular meanings and this can help to decode the meaning of the word.

Suffix	Meaning	Example
-able, -ible	capable of	readable, legible
-ain, -an	one connected	chaplain, artisan
-ance, -ence	state of	hesitance, difference
-ant	one who	applicant
-el, -et, -ette	little	parcel, pocket, statuette
-er, -eer, -ier	one who	butcher, auctioneer, collier
-ess	female	actress, princess
-fy	to make	pacify
-icle, -sel	small	article, morsel
-less	without	hopeless
-ling	little	gosling
-ment	state of being	encouragement
-ock	little	hummock
-oon, -on	large	balloon
-ory	place for	repository
-ous	full of	curious

A thesaurus (plural thesauri) aims to provide words that are similar in meaning – synonyms – in groups. Opposites – antonyms – are sometimes included alongside. *Roget's Thesaurus*, originally published in 1852, was created as the first analysis of the English language structured in this thematic way. To use this type of thesaurus, you look up your original word in an index at the back, which provides a series of numbered sub-groupings with different allied meanings and word types (chiefly nouns, adjectives, adverbs and verbs). Choose the most appropriate, and then look up the numbered group within the main text, to find a listing of synonyms and antonyms. The principles of the original thesaurus have been continued in modern versions, but several publishers now produce A-Z versions. These types are generally more user-friendly than the original Roget-style thesaurus. Figure 15.3 illustrates an example of a thesaurus entry.

Electronic thesauri

Some word-processing packages include a thesaurus. Place the cursor on the word you want to look up; click on the thesaurus function on the toolbar and this will present options to expand your search. These types of thesauri do not usually explain the meaning of a word.

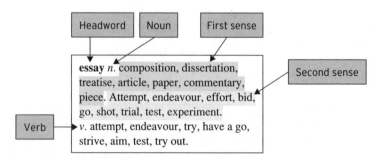

Figure 15.3 Example of a thesaurus entry.
Source: The Penguin A-Z Thesaurus, 1986. Harmondsworth: Penguin Books.

→ Specialist dictionaries

There is a range of specialist dictionaries that might be useful to you (see also Table 15.3):

- **Subject dictionary:** gives meanings of specialist terms within a discipline. It gives a quick reference to explanations of specialist terms that are not found in general dictionaries.

- **Spelling dictionary:** gives correct spellings as well as frequently misspelt versions with the correct spelling alongside.

- **Etymological dictionary:** gives the linguistic origins of words, and developments in their meaning.

- **Collocation dictionary:** gives words that are often positioned together. This is useful when you find yourself searching for one word usually used alongside another.

- **Rhyming dictionary:** gives words with similar end sounds; useful when writing poetry.

- **Pronunciation dictionary:** gives a phonetic version of the headword. You can work out the phonetic code from the symbols that are given, usually at the front of the dictionary.

- **Bilingual dictionary:** gives equivalent words from two languages, often arranged in two sections, translating from one language to the other, and vice versa.

- **English learner's dictionary:** primarily intended for those learning English as a second language, but very useful for all because they give examples of use, including idioms, and a pronunciation guide.

---

smart tip

Keep your writing as intelligible as possible

Each discipline has its own language, which is comprehensible to insiders; remember that one person's professional vocabulary or jargon can exclude others from understanding. Try to keep 'jargon' words to a minimum when you are writing. You can do this by using dictionaries and thesauri to help you find words that are close in meaning to the word(s) that were your first choice. This will enable you to be precise and professional in your use of language, while keeping your text clear and to the point.

Table 15.3 Different types of dictionaries and thesauri

Standard dictionary Dictionaries vary widely in size of content and in price; buying a good one is a sound investment	Subject dictionary Most libraries will stock at least one subject dictionary in your discipline
Features • Arranged in alphabetical order • At the most basic, gives pronunciations, meanings and different forms of the word • Some give examples of how the word is used in a sentence • May provide information about the origin of the word **Comments** • Some provide lists of foreign words used in English • May also include additional miscellany section giving, for example, information about weights and measures, acronyms and abbreviations	**Features** • Quick reference to explanations of specialist terms that you will not find in general dictionaries • Often provides guidance on pronunciation of terms and examples of usage • May give guidance on how to use a term in a sentence **Comments** • If you can afford it, a subject dictionary is a good investment: it will be something you will use throughout your student career
Online dictionary Usually available via university library website, but only with password because of licensing agreements	**Hand-held electronic dictionary** Wide price range. You may be allowed to use these in exams if you are a registered dyslexic student.
Features • Gives pronunciations, meanings, different forms of the word, information about the origin of the word and examples of how to use the word **Comments** • Immediately accessible • The *Oxford English Dictionary* (*OED*) provides British English spelling and usage • The *Merriam-Webster Dictionary* provides American English spelling and usage	**Features** • Access to the required word by typing letters on keypad • Provides alternative meanings and word forms • Through thesaurus function, gives antonyms and synonyms • Some may give pronunciation information **Comments** • It is probably better to opt for one that has a word database from a recognised dictionary publisher

Table 15.3 continued

Thesaurus	Computer software package dictionary and thesaurus functions
Features • Provides synonyms (sometimes also antonyms)	**Features** • Place the cursor on the word you want to look up; click on the thesaurus function on the toolbar and this will present options to expand your search
Comments • Principles of the original thesaurus have been continued in some modern versions but some publishers favour A–Z formats; these latter types are generally more user-friendly than the traditional Roget-style thesaurus	**Comments** • A software thesaurus does not usually explain the meaning of the word; it simply gives you synonyms and antonyms

Practical tips for developing your use of academic terms and language

Find out what the abbreviations mean in your dictionary and thesaurus. Look for the section on 'how to use this reference book', as this will explain the symbols and abbreviations that have been used. Knowing these will save you time and will help you to get the most out of the reference source you are using. For example, you can find out the pronunciation of terms from a special table.

Sign up for 'word of the day'. Some online dictionaries sites have a free sign-up feature that means you will receive a new word by e-mail every day. While some of these words may be totally unusable as far as you are concerned, many will add to your working vocabulary. Two examples of sites that have this facility are:

http://dictionary.reference.com/wordoftheday

http://www.m-w.com/cgi-bin/mwwod.plv

Consult a dictionary and thesaurus while you are writing. The best time to pick up new words and check on their meanings is when you are writing. You should try to get into the habit of looking up either of these reference works any time you feel unsure about any word or its use.

15.1 Find out what dictionaries and thesauri are available at your library. Explore the reference section to discover what general dictionaries are available. Have a look at several to see what information they give under the headwords. If you are thinking of buying a general dictionary for yourself, this is a good way of evaluating different types before you buy.

15.2 Create an instant personal glossary. Table 15.4 illustrates a personal glossary. You can create a quick, fold-away version by taking a sheet of A4 paper and folding it into 24 squares. This can act as a portable ready reference for adding new words as a tool for active learning when you are reading or revising.

15.3 Take the 'University Word List' and 'Academic Word List' challenges. English-language researchers have produced lists of words most commonly used in academic texts.

- The 'University Word List' comprises more than 800 words divided into 11 categories, with those in list 1 being the most frequently used, those in list 11 being those used less frequently. This list can be found on: **http://jbauman.com/ UWL.html**

- The 'Academic Word List' represents a further appraisal of academic vocabulary and comprises more than 500 words. These words can be found on: **http://www.auburn.edu/ ~nunnath/engl6240/wlistuni.html**

Look at these lists and challenge yourself to find out the meanings of any word that is not familiar to you; record the word and its meaning in your personal glossary.

Table 15.4 Example of a basic personal glossary. You can use this type of 'quick glossary' for recording meanings or simply as a spellchecking list. If you have a lot of specialist terms to learn, then you might want to create a quick glossary for each subject or even topic. This can then be filed along with the relevant notes. In a very short time, you will have expanded your vocabulary considerably and will be able to use your glossary words correctly in your academic writing. Being more familiar with some of the terms and their meanings will also help to speed up your reading.

A antonym: word opposite in meaning	B	C	D derivation: origin, tracing, word root	E	F
G glossary: word list	H headword: key word for a dictionary entry	I	J	K	L
M	N	O	P phonetic: by pronunciation prefix: put at the beginning	Q	R
S suffix: put at the end synonym: word similar in meaning	T	U	V	W	X Y Z

Editing
and
revision

16 | Reviewing, editing and proof-reading

How to make sure your writing is concise and correct

Looking critically at your own writing is essential if you want to produce work of the highest quality. These editing skills will allow you to improve the sense, grammar and syntax of your written assignments.

Key topics:
- → The reviewing, editing and proof-reading process
- → Reviewing your answers in exams
- → The value of reviewing, editing and proof-reading

Key terms
Annotate   Syntax   Typo   *Vice versa*

Writing is a process. It begins with a plan and it finishes with reviewing, editing and proof-reading. This means that you should read your text critically before submitting it for assessment. The effort you invest in this final stage will contribute to the quality of your work and to your assessed mark. Ideally, you should leave a gap of time between completing the writing and beginning the reviewing process, as this allows you to 'distance' yourself from the work and helps you look at it as a new reader would.

→ The reviewing, editing and proof-reading process

At this stage you are performing the role of editor. This means that you are looking critically at your text for content, relevance and sense, as well as for flaws in layout, grammar, punctuation and spelling. You should also check for consistency in all aspects, for example, in the use of terminology, in spelling, and in presentational features such as font and point size, layout of paragraphs, and labelling of tables and diagrams.

Clearly, there are a lot of aspects to cover, and some degree of overlap in different parts of the process. Some people prefer to go through their text in one sweep, amending any flaws as they go; others, in particular professional writers, take a staged approach, reading through their text several times looking at a different facet each time.

Definitions

Reviewing: appraising critically; that is, examining an essay or assignment to ensure that it meets the requirements and objectives of the task and that the overall sense is conveyed well.

Editing: revising and correcting later drafts of an essay or assignment, to arrive at a final version. Usually, this involves the smaller rather than the larger details, such as details of punctuation, spelling, grammar and layout.

Proof-reading: checking a printed copy for errors of any sort.

There are five aspects to consider in the reviewing process:

- content and relevance
- clarity, style and coherence
- grammatical correctness
- spelling and punctuation
- presentation.

Table 16.1 provides a quick checklist of key aspects to consider under each of these themes. This has been designed for photocopying so that you can, if you wish, use it as a checklist each time you complete a piece of work. Table 16.2 gives some helpful strategies you can adopt when going through the editing process.

Professional proof-readers have developed a system of symbols to speed up the editing and proof-reading process. You may wish to adopt some of these yourself, and you are certainly likely to see some of them, and other 'informal' marks, on work returned by tutors. Table 16.3 illustrates some of the more commonly used symbols.

Table 16.1 **Proof-reading and editing checklists.** Each heading represents a 'sweep' of your text, checking for the aspects shown. The text is assumed to be a piece of writing produced for assessment. This table is copyright-free for use when reviewing your work.

Content and relevance
❏ The intent of the instruction word has been followed
❏ The question or task has been completed, that is, you have answered all sections or required numbers of questions
❏ The structure is appropriate
❏ The text shows objectivity
❏ The examples are relevant
❏ All sources are correctly cited
❏ The facts presented are accurate

Clarity, style and coherence
❏ The aims and objectives are clear
❏ What you wrote is what you meant to write
❏ The text is fluent, with appropriate use of signpost words
❏ Any informal language has been removed
❏ The style is academic and appropriate for the task
❏ The content and style of each section is consistent
❏ The tense used in each section is suited to the time frame of your text and is consistent
❏ The length of the text sections are balanced appropriately

Grammatical correctness
❏ All sentences are complete
❏ All sentences make sense
❏ Paragraphs have been correctly used
❏ Suggestions made by grammar checker have been accepted/rejected
❏ Text has been checked against your own checklist of recurrent errors
❏ Text is consistent in adopting either British or American English

Spelling and punctuation
❏ Any blatant 'typos' have been corrected by reading for meaning
❏ Text has been spellchecked or read through carefully for spelling
❏ A check has been made for spelling of subject-specific and foreign words
❏ Punctuation has been checked, if possible, by the 'reading aloud' method
❏ Proper names are correctly capitalised
❏ Overlong sentences have been divided

Presentation
❏ If no word-count target is given, the overall length will depend on the amount of time you were given to complete the task. Ask your tutor, if you're uncertain
❏ The text length meets the word-count target – neither too short nor too long
❏ Overall neatness checked
❏ The cover-sheet details and presentation aspects are as required
❏ The bibliography/reference list is correctly formatted
❏ Page numbers have been included (in position stipulated, if given)
❏ The figures and tables are in appropriate format

Table 16.2 Editing strategies. The reviewing/editing/proof-reading process can be done in a single 'sweep'. As you become more experienced, you will become adept at doing this. However, initially, it might help you to focus on each of these three broad aspects in a separate 'sweep' of the text. Note that the first two sections combine pairs of aspects considered in Table 16.1. Further discussion of presentational issues is provided in **Ch 19**.

Content and relevance; clarity, style and coherence
• Read text aloud - your ears will help you to identify errors that your eyes have missed
• Revisit the task or question. Check your interpretation against the task as set
• Work on a hard copy using editing symbols to correct errors
• Identify that the aims you set out in your introduction have been met
• Read objectively and assess whether the text makes sense. Look for inconsistencies in argument
• Check that all your facts are correct
• Insert additional or overlooked evidence that strengthens the whole
• Remove anything that is not relevant or alter the text so that it is clear and unambiguous. Reducing text by 10-25 per cent can improve quality considerably
• Critically assess your material to ensure that you have attributed ideas to the sources, that is, check that you have not committed plagiarism
• Remodel any expressions that are too informal for academic contexts
• Eliminate gendered or discriminatory language

Grammatical correctness, spelling and punctuation
• Check titles and subtitles are appropriate to the style of the work and stand out by using bold or underlining (not both)
• Consider whether the different parts link together well - if not, introduce signpost words to guide the reader through the text
• Check for fluency in sentence and paragraph structure - remodel as required
• Check sentence length - remodel to shorter or longer sentences. Sometimes shorter sentences are more effective than longer ones
• Ensure that you have been consistent in spelling conventions, for example, following British English rather than American English spelling or *vice versa*
• Spelling errors - use the spellchecker but be prepared to double-check in a standard dictionary if you are in doubt or cannot find a spelling within the spellchecker facility
• Check for cumbersome constructions - divide or restructure sentence(s); consider whether active or passive is more suitable. Consider using vocabulary that might convey your point more eloquently
• Check for use of 'absolute' terms to ensure that you maintain objectivity

Table 16.2 continued

Presentation
• Check that you have made good use of white space, that is, not crammed the text into too tight a space, and that your text is neat and legible
• If your text is word-processed, check that you have followed standard typing conventions. Follow any 'house style' rules stipulated by your department
• Check that you have included a reference list, consistently following a recognised method, and that all citations in the text are matched by an entry in the reference list and vice versa
• Ensure all pages are numbered and are stapled or clipped, and, if appropriate, ensure that the cover page is included
• Check that your name, matriculation number and course number are included. You may wish to add this information as a footnote that appears on each page
• Ensure question number and title are included
• Check that labelling of diagrams, charts and other visual material is in sequence and consistently presented
• Ensure that supporting material is added in sequence as appendices, footnotes, endnotes or as a glossary as applicable

Technical notes

The word processor has made the reviewing and editing task much easier. Here are some tips for using this software effectively:

■ Use the word-count facility to check on length.

■ Use the 'View' facility to check page breaks and general layout before you print out.

■ Use the facilities within the 'Format' menu to control presentational aspects like paragraph spacing, tabs for indents and styles for bulleted and numbered lists.

■ Use the spell- and grammar-checkers to guide you, but do not rely on them 100 per cent as they are fallible.

■ Sometimes the grammar checker will announce that you have used the passive voice. This is often a standard academic usage and, therefore, is not an error.

■ Sometimes staff add comments to students' work using 'Tools/Track Changes' on the Microsoft Word software. Depending on the version you are using, feedback information can usually be accepted or rejected by right-clicking on the word or punctuation point that has been marked for alteration.

Table 16.3 Common proof-reading symbols. University lecturers and tutors use a variety of symbols on students' assignments to indicate errors, corrections or suggestions. These can apply to punctuation, spelling, presentation or grammar. The symbols provide a kind of 'shorthand' that acts as a code to help you see how you might be able to amend your text so that it reads correctly and fluently. In this table some of the more commonly used correction marks are shown alongside their meanings. The sample text shows how these symbols may be used either in the text or the margin to indicate where a change is recommended.

Correction mark	Meaning	Example
⌐ (np)	(new) paragraph	*Text* *margin*
≠	change CAPITALS to small letters (lower case)	The correction marks that tutors
~~	change into **bold** type	use in students' texts are generally
≡	change into CAPITALS	made to help identify where there
⌒	close up (delete space)	have been errors of spelling or ʌe/ʌg
/ or ❧ or ⊢	delete	punctuation. They can ~~often~~ (STET)
⋏	insert a word or letter	indicate where there is lack of
Y	insert space	paragraphing or grammatical
.... or (STET)	leave unchanged	accuracy. If you find that work is (np)
Insert punctuation symbol in a circle (P)	punctuation	returned to you with such
plag.	plagiarism	marks correction, then it is ⊔⊓
→	run on (no new paragraph)	worthwhile spending some time
Sp.	spelling	analysing the common errors as ❧
⊔⊓	transpose text	well as the comments, because this
?	what do you mean?	will help you to improve the
??	text does not seem to make sense	quality of presentation and content
✓	good point/correct	of your work this reviewing can ⊙/≡
✗	error	have a positive effect on your
		assessed mark.
		In the margin, the error symbols are separated by a slash (/) if there is more than one per line.

→ Reviewing your answers in exams

For essays written in exams, the reviewing process has to be swift
and efficient (**Ch 21**). Here, you will normally have time only to
skim-read the text, making adjustments as you go. If you find you
have missed something out, place an insert mark (Λ or $\curlywedge$) in the
text and/or margin with the annotation 'see additional paragraph x';
then write this paragraph, clearly identified, at the end of the answer
(where you will have left space for just this contingency). Similarly,
if you have consistently made an error, for example, referred to
Louis XIV throughout as Louis XVI, then just put an asterisk beside the
first occurrence of the error and a note at the end of your answer or
in the margin 'Consistent error. Please read as "XIV" '. You will not
lose any marks for correcting your work in these ways.

→ The value of reviewing, editing and proof-reading

Although the editing process may seem tedious and more complex
than it might have appeared at first, a text that is not revised in
this way will be unlikely to receive as favourable a reading – and
possibly as high a mark – as one that has been fully reviewed, edited
and proofed. It is the mix of style, content, structure and presentation
that will gain you marks, and anything you can do to increase your
'mark-earning' power will be to your advantage. In the longer term,
learning how to edit your work properly will help you to develop a
skill of critical analysis that will stand you in good stead throughout
your career.

Practical tips for reviewing, editing and proof-reading your work

Make time for checking. When planning the writing of an essay or
assignment, ensure that you have allowed adequate time for reviewing
and proof-reading. You don't want to spoil all your hard work by
skimping on the final stage. Leave some time between finishing the
final draft and returning to check the whole text, because you will
return to your work with a fresh and possibly more critical eye.

Work from a hard copy. Reading through your work laid out on paper, which is the format in which your marker will probably see it, will help you identify errors and inconsistencies more readily than might be possible on the screen. A paper version is also easier to annotate (although this can also be done using the 'Track Changes' facility on your word processor). A printout also allows you to see the whole work in overview, and focus on the way the text 'flows'. If necessary, spread it out on the desk in front of you.

Follow the 'reading aloud' check. This is a tried and tested technique to ensure that what you have written actually makes sense. Simply read your text aloud to yourself. Your ears will hear the errors that your eyes might miss on a silent reading of the text. This will help you correct grammatical and spelling inconsistencies, as well as punctuation omissions. (Note: for obvious reasons, this method is not suitable for use in exams.)

Map your work to obtain an overview. 'Label' each paragraph with a topic heading and list these in a linear way on a separate paper. This will provide you with a 'snapshot' of your text and will allow you to appraise the order, check against any original plan, and adjust the position of parts as you feel necessary.

Check for relevance. Ensure that you have written and interpreted the question as set and have not 'made up' another title for the task. Whatever you have written will be judged by the terms of the original question, not by one that you have created.

Check for consistency in the elements of your text. For example, ensure that your introduction and conclusion complement and do not contradict each other.

Check for factual accuracy. Ensure that all the facts are correct, for example, in a history essay that the date sequences are consistent, or in a scientific paper that a numerical answer you have reached is realistic. It is very easy to type a date erroneously or make a final slip in the transposition of a number from one area of the page to another and, thus, lose marks.

Stick to your word limits/targets. Remember that too few words can be just as bad as too many. The key point is that your writing must be clear to your reader. Sometimes this means giving a longer explanation; sometimes it means simplifying what you have written. However, at this stage, if you are over the word-count limit, then check for ways in which you can reword the text to eliminate redundant words while maintaining the sense you intended to convey.

Create 'white space'. To help produce a more 'reader-friendly' document that will not deter the marker, try to create 'white space' by:

- leaving space (one 'return' space) between paragraphs;
- justifying only on the left side of the page;
- leaving space around diagrams, tables and other visual material; and
- leaving reasonable spaces between headings, sub-headings and text.

Check that all the 'secretarial' aspects are in place. Neat presentation, punctuation and spelling all help your reader to access the information, ideas and argument of your writing. While this may not gain you marks, it will certainly ensure that you do not lose marks even indirectly by making the marker struggle to 'decode' your work.

Check other visual aspects. Diagrams, tables and figures should be drawn using a ruler, if you cannot create these electronically. Only in some subjects would freehand drawing be acceptable, for example, in the study of Architecture.

GO And now . . .

16.1 Reflect on past submissions. Look at an essay or assignment that you have already submitted and go through it using the checklist in Table 16.1. Concentrate on two pages and, using a highlighter, mark all flaws, inconsistencies or errors. Look at the overall effect of these errors and reflect on the extent to which this may have lost you marks; then consider how you might allow for more time for the editing/proof-reading phase next time round.

16.2 Practise using the standard proof-reading marks. On the same piece of text, insert the relevant standard proof-reading symbols (Table 16.3) on the text and in the margin. Learning how to use these symbols will help you speed up the proof-reading process.

▶

16.3 Practise condensing a piece of text. This is an acknowledged way of improving your work, though you have to bear in mind any word targets that have been set. Look at your text for irrelevant points, wordy phrases, repetitions and excessive examples; if you can reduce its original length by 10–25 per cent, you will probably find that you have created a much tighter, easier-to-read piece of writing.

Plagiarism
and
referencing

Plagiarism and copyright infringement

How to avoid being accused of 'stealing' the ideas and work of others

Many students have only a vague understanding of plagiarism and copyright issues. However, failing to take account of them means you may risk loss of marks and serious disciplinary action. This chapter provides an insight into what both types of infringement involve.

Key topics:

→ What is plagiarism?
→ What is copyright infringement?

Key terms
Copyright   Paraphrase   Plagiarism   Synonym   Verbatim

Plagiarism and copyright are two related topics that are extremely important academically and legally, but which are often misunderstood by students. They have become more significant in recent years due to technological advances such as digital scanners, photocopiers and electronic file exchange, which make it simple to 'cut and paste' and copy materials. This means it is easier to commit an offence unknowingly. You need to be fully aware of the issues involved so you can acknowledge intellectual property appropriately and avoid losing marks or being involved in further disciplinary action.

→ What is plagiarism?

Plagiarism can be defined as: 'the unacknowledged use of another's work as if it were one's own' (University of Dundee, 2005).

Alongside other forms of academic dishonesty, universities regard intentional plagiarism as a very serious offence. The regulations normally prescribe a range of penalties depending on the severity of the case, from a simple reduction in marks, to the ultimate sanctions of exclusion from the university or refusal to award a degree. You will find the exact penalties for your institution specified in departmental or school handbooks.

Punishments for copying

Copying an essay or other piece of work by a fellow student (past or present) is cheating. The punishment is often an assessment mark of zero *for both parties*, and further disciplinary measures may be taken. If you let someone copy your work, you are regarded as just as culpable as the 'real' cheat – so consider the risk to your academic future if you misguidedly allow someone to copy your work.

Plagiarism is thus something to be avoided, and it is assumed that no one would deliberately set out to cheat in this way. The problem is that it is easy to plagiarise unwittingly. Regarding such 'unintentional plagiarism', you should note the following:

- The concept of 'work' in the definition of plagiarism given above includes ideas, writing or inventions, and not simply words.
- The notion of 'use' in the definition does not only mean 'word for word' (an exact copy) but also 'in substance' (a paraphrase of the notions involved).
- Use of another's work *is* acceptable, *if* you acknowledge the source.

The first two of these aspects give an indication of the potential dangers for students, but the third provides a remedy. To avoid the risk of unintentional plagiarism, adopt the following advice: if you think a particular author has said something particularly well, then quote them directly *and* provide a reference to the relevant article or book beside the quote. Note that the convention in academic writing is to use inverted commas (and sometimes italics) to signify clearly that a quotation is being made. The reference or citation is generally given in one of several standard forms that are discussed in Table 18.1. For examples of plagiarism, see Table 17.1.

Examples of plagiarism are given in Table 17.1. Each aspect of plagiarism is explained and a suggestion is made for an acceptable method of paraphrasing the material used.

examples with revisions and explains exactly what the grounds for the charge of plagiarism are. In all cases each citation would be included in the reference list at the end of the text. Explanations for several points made in the Comments column are given in **Ch 18**.

Category of plagiarism	Example	Revision or suggestion	Comment
Case study 1 Not giving credit to the source at all	*Danny has used material direct from the source without any acknowledgement. This is perceived as blatant plagiarism.*		
	Original: Most road accidents are alcohol-related: 50% are fatalities but not necessarily of those under alcoholic influence (Annual Police Statistics, 2004, in Milne, 2006). Danny's text: The majority of road accidents are alcohol-related and 50% of these cases result in a death, but not always of the person who has consumed the alcohol.	Revision: A study of police statistics by Milne (2006) reported that approximately half of road accidents result in a death because one of the parties involved has been under the influence of alcohol.	Danny has rearranged the order slightly without noting the source of the data that he cites. Plagiarism aside, he's not explained how these figures were derived and hence they are represented as hearsay rather than hard fact.
Case study 2 Word substitution with some minor re-ordering of the original	*Xi thinks he can avoid plagiarism by changing odd words and word order of the original text. That is still considered to be plagiarism.*		
	Original: Post-operative physiotherapy is vital to the improvement in the quality of life of the elderly patient (Kay, 2003). Xi's version: Therapy after surgery is critical to the recovery of the older patient and their quality of life (Kay, 2003).	Revision: Kay (2003) attributes the improved quality of life levels of elderly patients who have undergone surgery to physiotherapy treatment.	Xi has used a thesaurus to find synonyms and has reversed two points. This does not show understanding of the issue. The revision uses the verb 'attributes' to indicate that this is a claim made by Kay, but is not necessarily a view shared by the author reporting it.
Case study 3 Using words from text and inserting citation, but omitting quotation marks	*Eileen's quoted the exact words from the original text. She has cited the source but has not inserted the quotation marks. However, this is still plagiarism.*		
	Original: It could be assumed that undergraduate students wrote what they could write and not what they actually know. Eileen's version: Sim (2006) asserted that students wrote what they could write and not what they actually know.	Revision: Sim (2006) asserted that students 'wrote what they could and not what they actually know'.	Although she has cited the source, by lifting the exact words taken from the text she is only doing half the job. She must place the exact words within inverted commas (quotation marks) (see p. 193).

Table 17.1 continued

Category of plagiarism	Example	Revision or suggestion	Comment
Case study 4 Using words from text and inserting quotation marks but omitting the citation	*Ed's copied the words from the original text and placed these within inverted commas but has not sourced the quotes. This, too, is a form of **plagiarism**.* Original: It could be assumed that undergraduate students wrote what they could write and not what they actually know. Ed's version: Essentially, what was noted was that the students 'wrote what they could write and not what they actually know'.	Revision: Essentially, it was noted that students 'wrote what they could write and not what they actually know' (Sim, 2006). Or Sim (2006) noted that students 'wrote what they could write and not what they actually know'.	Although he has put in the inverted commas, by not including the source , Ed has failed to give recognition to the intellectual property of Sim. Furthermore, he has failed to understand that the citation brings credibility to his own work.
Case study 6 Stringing together a series of direct quotations with very little input from the student.	*Sally's struggling to understand her subject and lacks confidence in her own writing abilities. She tends to do more and more reading and picks out the bits she thinks are relevant. She puts those bits that seem to be related together in the same paragraph. She adds the sources and hopes that this evidences her understanding because she has clearly read widely. This does not reflect her understanding of the ideas that she is using to illustrate her argument. This is poor academically, and could also be considered to be **plagiarism**.* Sally's version: Brown (2000) noted 'insomnia is the ailment of the elderly'. Smith (2004) stated 'insomnia is a function of stressful living'. Jones (2001) said 'insomnia is a figment of those who sleep for an average of 5 hours a night'. This means that insomnia is a problem.	Revision: Perceptions about the incidence of insomnia are varied. Insomnia is problematic for the elderly (Brown, 2000) and for the stressed (Smith, 2004). However, Jones (2001) contends that people who claim to be insomniacs actually sleep for an average of 5 hours per night. This suggests that insomnia is often a perception rather than a reality.	Sally has created a kind of 'shopping list' of sources, but her list does not make the connection between the explicit point about types of people who suffer insomnia and the implicit point that those who claim insomnia do not actually suffer from it. Often students string together citations like this without making the underpinning connections or interpretations.

Case study 7 Downloading from the internet by cutting and pasting.	*Jeff has done the prescribed reading and has produced a piece of text that seems slightly too good when compared with the rest of what he has written. The hypertext links suggest that the words are not his own. There is no citation. This is an example of **Internet plagiarism**.*	
	Jeff's version: The incidence of drug misuse is something that invites action from international agencies including the <u>WHO</u>. There are also <u>European organisations</u> that have recognised the need to counter drug trafficking as well as establishing drug rehabilitation regimens throughout the European theatre.	Jeff's use of this text shows that he has not processed the material. Apart from his reliance on a source that may not be robust in that there is no certainty that his source is monitored or authenticated, he has shown that he has not engaged with the literature from more academic sources.
	Revision: International and European organisations have engaged in tackling drug trafficking, misuse, and rehabilitation. (www.drugfree.org accessed 1.1.07)	
Case study 8 'Sharing' (copying?) work created with another student	*Marie has worked closely with her student buddy, Tim. They've shared material and both have included the same diagram which is a product of their collaboration. No explanation has been given. This is **plagiarism**.*	
	Marie's version: Figure 3 shows that . . . (diagram inserted) Tim's version: Figure 3 illustrates that . . . (diagram inserted)	Suggested strategy: It is good to work with a buddy to discuss and sketch the diagram. However, for the final version, both parties should work independently and should acknowledge the contribution of their partner, at an appropriate point, either in the text, the figure legend, the acknowledgements, or the reference list.

Cutting and pasting

The practice of cutting (copying) and pasting electronically (for example, taking material from websites) and using this in an essay without citing it, is regarded as plagiarism and will be punished if detected. Universities now have sophisticated electronic means of identifying where this has occurred.

What constitutes acceptable paraphrasing?

Good paraphrasing involves a significant re-write of the original that retains the meaning and possibly adds extra points. Look particularly at the reporting words (**Ch 18**). Poor paraphrasing, which may be considered plagiarism (Table 17.1), involves merely changing the odd word or reconfiguring the order of the words.

Three good reasons for paraphrasing

- It shows you understand the concepts and ideas from the original text.
- It gives your reader a broad idea of the key ideas or arguments without having to read all the source material.
- It demonstrates your capacity for critical thinking.

→ What is copyright infringement?

Copyright law 'gives the creators of a wide range of material, such as literature, art, music, sound recordings, films and broadcasts economic rights' (The UK Intellectual Property Office, 2007). Copyright infringement is regarded as equivalent to stealing, and legal rights are sometimes jealously guarded by companies with the resources to prosecute.

In the UK, authors have literary copyright over their material for their life, and their estate has copyright for a further 70 years. Publishers have typographical copyright for 25 years. This is why the copyright symbol © is usually accompanied by a date and the owner's name. You'll find this information on the publication details page at the start of a book.

You will be at risk of breaking the law if you copy (for example, photocopy, digitally scan or print out) material to which someone else owns the copyright, unless you have their express permission, or unless the amount you copy falls within the limits accepted for 'fair dealing'.

'Educational copying', *for non-commercial private study or research*, is sometimes allowed by publishers (they will state this on the material, and may allow multiple copies to be made). Otherwise, for single copies *for private study or research*, you should only copy what would fall under the 'fair dealing' provision, for which there is no precise definition in law.

Private study or research

This means what it says: the limits discussed here apply to that use and not to commercial or other uses, such as photocopying an amusing article for your friends. Copying of software and music CDs (including 'sharing' of MP3 files) is usually illegal, although you are usually permitted to make a *personal* back-up copy of a track or CD you already own.

Established practice suggests that you should photocopy no more than 5 per cent of the work involved, or:

- one chapter of a book;
- one article per volume of an academic journal;
- 20 per cent (to a maximum of 20 pages) of a short book;
- one poem or short story (maximum of 10 pages) from an anthology;
- one separate illustration or map up to A4 size (note: illustrations that are parts of articles and chapters may be included in the allowances noted above);
- short excerpts of musical works – not whole works or movements (note: copying of any kind of public performance is not allowed without permission).

Approved copyright exceptions

Some copying for academic purposes may be licensed by the Copyright Licensing Agency (CLA) on behalf of authors. Other electronically distributed material may be licensed through the HERON (Higher Education Resources On-Demand) scheme. In these cases you may be able to copy or print out more than the amounts listed here, including multiple copies. Your university may also 'buy in' to licensing schemes, such as those offered by the NLA (Newspaper Licensing Agency) and the Performing Rights Society. As these can refer to very specific sources, consult your library's staff if in doubt.

These limits apply to single copies – you can't take multiple copies of any of the above items, or pass on a single copy for multiple copying to someone else, who may be in ignorance of the source or of specific or general copyright issues.

In legal terms, it doesn't matter whether you paid for the source or not: copyright is infringed when the whole or a substantial part is copied without permission – and 'substantial' here can mean a qualitatively significant section even if this is a small part of the whole.

The same rules apply to printing or copying material on the Web unless the author gives explicit (i.e. written) clearance. This applies to copying images as well as text from the Internet, although a number of sites do offer copyright-free images. A statement on the author's position on copying may appear on the home page or a page linked directly from it.

Complexity of copyright law

Note that the material in this chapter is a summary, and much may depend on individual circumstances.

Practical tips for avoiding plagiarism

Avoid copying material by electronic means. You may only do this if you are prepared to quote the source. If you use the material in your work, and fail to add an appropriate citation, this would be regarded as cheating.

When making notes, always write down your sources. You may risk plagiarising if you cannot recall or find the source of a piece of text. Avoid this by getting into the habit of making a careful note of the source on the same piece of paper that you used to summarise or copy it out. Always use quote marks ('. . .') when taking such notes verbatim from texts and other materials, to indicate that what you have written down is a *direct copy* of the words used, as you may forget this at a later time. You do not need to quote directly in the final version of your work, but if you paraphrase you should still cite the source.

Try not to paraphrase another person's work too closely. Taking key phrases and rearranging them, or merely substituting some words with synonyms is still regarded as plagiarism.

Follow the academic custom of quoting sources. You should do this even if you prefer to use your own wording rather than a direct copy of the original. The reference to the source signifies that you are making that statement on the basis of the ideas reported there. If you are unclear about the different methods of mentioning sources and constructing a reference list, consult **Ch 18**.

Avoid overuse of quotations. Plagiarism still occurs if a considerable percentage of your assignment is comprised of quotations. In general, quotations should be used sparingly.

Double-check on your 'original' ideas. If you have what you think is a novel idea, do not simply accept that your brainwave is unique. It's common for people to forget the original source of an idea, which may resurface in their mind after many years and perhaps in a different context – this may have happened to you. Think carefully about possible sources that you may have forgotten about; ask others (such as your tutor or supervisor) whether they have come across the idea before; and consult relevant texts, encyclopaedias or the Web.

17.1 Double-check your department's (or university's) plagiarism policy. This should spell out the precise situations in which you might break rules. It may also give useful information on the department's preferred methods for citing sources.

17.2 Next time you are in the library, read the documentation about photocopying (often displayed beside the photocopiers). This will provide detailed information about current legislation and any local exceptions.

17.3 Modify your note-taking technique. Put any direct transcriptions in quotes and add full details of the source whenever you take notes from a textbook or paper source.

18 | Citing and listing references

How to refer appropriately to the work of others

The convention in academic writing at all levels is that you must support your discussion of a topic by referring to the relevant literature. There are several methods in use and which one you will be required to adopt will depend on the conventions within your discipline. This chapter outlines four of the more common styles showing you how to reference your source in text and how to list these in your reference list or bibliography.

Key topics:
→ Why you need to cite your sources
→ Using information within your text
→ How to cite the work in the text
→ Different reference methods

Key terms
Bibliography   Citation   Ellipsis   Ibid.   Indentation   Op. cit.
Reference list   Superscript

When you write any kind of academic paper – an essay, a report, a dissertation or a thesis – you are expected to give the sources of information and ideas you have drawn from your in-depth reading on the subject (**Ch 10** and **Ch 17**). This means that you have to give your reader sufficient information to be able to locate your source. This is done in the body of the text at the point where you refer to (cite) the source. You then give full details of it either in a footnote, endnote or separate reference list at the end of the paper.

Methods vary (see Table 18.1), and the preferred referencing method for your discipline will be stipulated in your course handbook, or may be recommended by your lecturer or supervisor. However, you must be able to recognise the alternative styles in order to interpret the information given. If you are unable to obtain style guide information, then seek the help of a librarian. Your library website may also provide useful links.

Table 18.1 **Choosing a referencing style.** Departments normally specify the referencing style. Where no guidance is given, then the choice is up to you. This table shows the most significant features, advantages and disadvantages of four common styles used in all forms of academic writing, including undergraduate and postgraduate assignments. It applies to all forms of writing – from essays to theses.

Harvard	
Features	• **Name/date** system used in the text (page number included only if making a reference to a specific quote or data) • Name of author can be included as part of the sentence (date in round brackets immediately after the name) *or* • Name and date both placed in round brackets at the end of the sentence
Advantages	• Minimal typing: once-only entry in alphabetical order by author name in the reference list • Easy to identify contributors in a field from the citations shown in the text • Easy to make adjustments in the text and the reference list
Disadvantages	• Name/date references can be intrusive in text • Not well-suited to citing archive material, e.g. historical documents, which may not have full details sufficient to comply with the system
Modern Languages Association (MLA)	
Features	• **Name/page** system in text; date at end of reference • Name of author can be included as part of the sentence (page number comes in brackets at the end of the sentence or clause) *or* • Name and page number(s) (no punctuation) both placed in brackets at the end of the sentence
Advantages	• Minimal typing as details are printed only once in alphabetical order by author name in the reference list, which makes it easy to locate the source information • Easy to identify contributors in a field from the citations shown in the text
Disadvantages	• Date of publication of source not in the text and not immediately evident in the reference list because of the position at the end of the reference • Indentation in 'follow-on' lines in the reference list can give a 'ragged' appearance to the layout of the reference list

Table 18.1 continued

Vancouver	
Features	• **Numerical** system with full-size numerals in brackets after the reported point • If another reference is made to a source in the text, the second and subsequent references use the number given to the reference when it was used for the first time
Advantages	• Numbers are less intrusive in the text • Numbers are listed in numerical order at the end of the text, thus it is easy to locate the reference
Disadvantages	• No bibliographical information in the text, thus difficult to gauge significance of the sources • Cumbersome • Use of one number each time the source is used • Involves a considerable amount of checking and slows down the writing process
Chicago	
Features	• **Superscript numbers** used in the text • Relates superscript numbers to footnotes on the same page • Provides reference information in footnotes and reference list (note that the format differs between footnotes and reference list)
Advantages	• Numbering system is unobtrusive and does not interrupt the flow of the text • Use of *op. cit.* and *ibid.* in the referencing saves retyping of bibliographical information
Disadvantages	• First mention of a source gives full details, subsequent references give only name/page • More difficult to track the main contributors • Layout of footnote references differs from the bibliographical reference (if used) • Intensive checking to ensure that all superscript references are consistent after any changes

How should I cite and list my references?

Examples of the four conventions described in Table 18.1 are provided in Tables 18.2–18.5. It is important to follow one style consistently.

Definitions: listings

Bibliography: a listing at the end of your work of all books, journals, web and online materials that you have consulted as preparation for your paper. Note that you do not need to have referred to all these sources directly in your text.

Reference list: all the books, journals, web and online materials you have referred to in your paper. This list is usually at the end of the work. This is the more usual term for essay work.

→ Why you need to cite your sources

Academic convention requires you to give this information in order to:

● acknowledge the use of other people's work – you must demonstrate clearly where you have borrowed text or ideas from others; even if you cite an author's work in order to disagree with it, you have made use of their intellectual property and you must show that you recognise this (there is more explanation of intellectual property and plagiarism in **Ch 17**);

● help your readers understand how your argument/discussion was assembled and what influenced your thinking – this will help them form opinions about your work;

● help your reader/marker evaluate the extent of your reading. This may help them to assess your work and to advise you on further or more relevant reading;

● provide your readers with sufficient information to enable them to consult the source materials for themselves, if they wish; and

● ensure that you do not lose marks by failing to provide a reference list.

smart tip

Software referencing packages

These can be used to fit your reference list to any of several conventions. However, it is worth reflecting on whether it is good use of your time to learn how to use a relatively complex package and key in the data to 'feed' the package, when you could achieve a similar end result with common-sense use of a list typed straight into a word-processed table, which can then be sorted alphabetically.

Essentially there are two means by which you can introduce the work of others into your text – by *quoting* exact words from a source, or by *citation*, which involves paraphrasing the idea in your own words. In both instances you need to indicate the source material by means of the chosen style of citation (Table 18.1).

Quotation in the text

There are two possibilities. If the quotation is short, then the exact words are placed within single inverted commas within the sentence (e.g. xxxx 'zzzz zz zzzz zz zzzz' xxx). If you are using a longer quotation, usually 30 words or more, then no inverted commas are used. The status of the text as a quotation is indicated by the use of indentation where several lines quoted from another source are indented within your own text and in single-line spacing. If you deliberately miss out some words from the original, then the 'gap' is represented by three dots. This is called ellipsis. For example:

xxxxxxxx xxxxx xxxxx xxxx xxx xx xxxxxxxxx xxxx xx xxxxxx xx xx

xxxx xxxxxx:

> ... zzzz z zzzzzz zzzzzzz zzz zzzzzzz zzzz zz z zz zzzz z zzzz zz zzzzzzzzzz zzzzzzzzzzzzzzzz. (source)

xxxxxxx xxxx xxx xxxx xx xx xx xxxxxxxxx xxxxx xxxxxxx xxxxx

xxxxxxxxxxxxxxx.

Quoting within a quote

The convention of British English is to use single inverted commas to cover the whole quotation and double inverted commas (quotation marks) for the quotation within the quotation. For example, 'xxxxxx "zzzz" xxx'. The convention in American English is the opposite.

Definition: ellipsis

The three dots used to substitute for words that have been omitted from a quotation are often used at the beginning of a quote as in the example above, or where some information that is irrelevant to your point has been omitted for brevity. Obviously, you should not omit words that change the sense of the quotation. For example, omitting the word 'not' in the following quotation would entirely change its sense: 'The adoption of the Euro as the common currency of the EU is *not* universally acceptable'.

Footnotes and endnotes

In some disciplines, footnotes and endnotes, generally using superscript numbers, lead readers to the source information. However, in other subjects, footnotes and endnotes are used simply to provide additional information, commentary or points of discussion about the content of the text. Footnotes generally appear at the bottom of the page where the link appears; endnotes are recorded in number order at the end of the body of the work.

→ How to cite the work in the text

There are essentially two ways in which to do this: the information-prominent and author-prominent methods. These depend on the style of referencing you have elected to follow. Four commonly used styles are laid out in Tables 18.2-18.5. The broad principles are outlined below.

- **Information-prominent method.** Here the statement is regarded as being generally accepted within the field of study. For example:

  Children express an interest in books and pictures from an early age (Murphy, 1995).

- **Author-prominent method.** Here the author and date of publication form part of the construction of the sentence. This formulation can be used with appropriate reporting words (see information box above) to reflect a viewpoint. For example:

  Murphy (1995) claimed that children as young as six months are able to follow a simple story sequence.

→ Different reference methods

Reference methods evolve as technology and preferences alter. Publishers of journals have been particularly influential in dictating styles that should be adopted in their publications. This has had the result that, even in the most commonly used styles, there have been modifications to create variants of the original format. The following tables illustrate common methods:

- Harvard (Table 18.2)
- Modern Languages Association (Table 18.3)
- Vancouver (Table 18.4)
- Chicago (Table 18.5).

Practical tips for citing and listing references

Record the bibliographical detail routinely. However you copy your notes – electronically, by photocopy or by writing – ensure that you record all the necessary bibliographical information, or you will waste time later on backtracking to find it.

Compile your reference list as you go along. Keep a list of the works you have read. Simply create a table within your software package and type in the details immediately you cite the source in the text. Doing this from time to time as you write saves you having to embark on a marathon of typing at the completion of the task. You will need to make a decision about the reference style at an early stage.

Don't mix referencing systems. Whichever method you use, make sure you follow its conventions to the letter, including all punctuation details. When no guidance is given, consult Table 18.1 to evaluate the possibilities.

Source quotations. If you note down a quotation speculatively for later use, then make sure that you write down full reference details alongside it. Never rely on your memory for referencing. Check everything and write it all down.

Check the detail. Allow plenty of time for final checking.

(GO) And now . . .

18.1 Identify the recommended referencing style for your subjects. These may differ from one subject to another; one tutor to another. Go through your module handbooks and see what has been stated and how the various subjects differ. If no explicit information is given, then analyse the way that the list of books on your reading lists have been printed. Alternatively, look at a well-known journal in your discipline and identify the style used in the journal. Often, very clear guidelines are given in a section in journals under the heading of 'Guidelines for contributors', or similar. If you compare this with the examples in Tables 18.2–18.5, then you may be able to identify the method by name.

18.2 Look at textbooks or journal articles in your subject area to identify what method is appropriate for quotations. Identify whether making direct quotations is common. In many academic areas, quotation from sources would be rare, and you need to be aware of this.

18.3 Check out availability of software referencing packages in your university's systems. Your library or computing support service will probably be able to give you guidance on the availability and operation of these packages.

Table 18.2(a) Outline of the Harvard method for citing references. This referencing system has the advantage of being simpler, quicker and possibly more readily adjustable than other systems. It is used internationally in a wide range of fields and provides author and date information in the text. Note that there are various interpretations of the method. This one generally follows BS5605:1990.

How to cite the reference in the text	How to lay out the reference list or bibliography
The cause of European integration has been further hampered by the conflict between competing interests in a range of economic activities (Roche, 1993). However, Hobart and Lyon (2002) have argued that this is a symptom of a wider disharmony which has its roots in socio-economic divisions arising from differing cultural attitudes towards the concept of the market economy. Morrison *et al.* (2001) have identified 'black market' economic activity in post-reunification Germany as one which exemplified this most markedly. Scott (2004) suggests that the black economy which existed prior to reunification operated on strong market economy principles. However, Main (2003 cited in Kay, 2004) has supported the view that black market economies are not culture dependent. Statistics presented by Johannes (2000) suggest that, in the UK, as many as 23 per cent of the population are engaged at any one time in the black economy. European-wide statistics indicate that figures for participation in the black economy may be as high as 30 per cent (Brandt, 2001).	Brandt, K-H., 2001. *Working the system* [online]. Available from: http://www.hvn.ac.uk/econ/trickco.htm [accessed 1.4.01]. *Ferry Times*, 1999. Where the money moves. *Ferry Times*, 12 April, p. 24. Hobart, K. and Lyon, A., 2002. *Socio-economic divisions: the cultural impact*. London: Thames Press. Johannes, B., 2000. Functional economics. In M. Edouard ed., *The naked economy*. Cologne: Rhein Verlag, 2000, pp. 120–30. Kay, W., 2004. *The power of Europe*. Dover: Kentish Press. Morrison, F., Drake, C., Brunswick, M. and Mackenzie, V., 2001. *Europe of the nations*. Edinburgh: Lothian Press. Roche, P., 1993. *European economic integration*. London: Amazon Press. Saunders, C., ed., 1996. *The economics of reality*. Dublin: Shamrock Press. Scott, R., 2004. Informal integration: the case of the non-monitored economy. *Journal of European Integration Studies*, 3 (2), pp. 81–9.
Quotations in the text	
The movement of money within the so-called black economy is regarded by Finance Ministers in Europe as 'a success story they could emulate' (*Ferry Times*, 12.4.99). According to Saunders (1996, p. 82) 'black economies build businesses'.	

Table 18.2(b) How to list different types of source following the Harvard method

Type of source material	Basic format: author surname | author initial | date | title | place of publication | publisher
Book by one author	Roche, P., 1993. *European economic integration*. London: Amazon Press.
Book by two authors	Hobart, K. and Lyon, A., 2002. *Socio-economic divisions: the cultural impact*. London: Thames Press.
Book with more than three authors	Morrison, F., Drake, C., Brunswick, M. and Mackenzie, V., 2001. *Europe of the nations*. Edinburgh: Lothian Press.
Book under editorship	Saunders, C., ed., 1996. *The economics of reality*. Dublin: Shamrock Press.
Chapter in a book	Johannes, B., 2000. Functional economics. In M. Edouard ed., *The naked economy*. Cologne: Rhein Verlag, 2000, 120-30.
Secondary referencing – where the original text is not available and the reference relates to a citation in a text that you have read, refer to the latter	Kay, W., 2004. *The power of Europe*. Dover: Kentish Press.
Journal article	Scott, R., 2004. Informal integration: the case of the non-monitored economy. *Journal of European Integration Studies*, 3 (2), 81-9.
Newspaper article	*Ferry Times*, 1999. Where the money moves. *Ferry Times*, 12 April, p. 24.
Internet references including e-books	Brandt, K-H. 2001. *Working the system* [online]. Available from: http://www.hvn.ac.uk/econ/trickco.htm [accessed 1.4.01].
Internet references: e-journals	Ross, F., 2000. Coping with dementia. *Geriatric Medicine* [online], 5 (14). Available from: http://germed.ac.ic/archive00000555/[accessed 11.01.04].

Notes:

- In this version of the Harvard method only the first word of a title is capitalised. With the exception of proper nouns, other words are in lower case. Each entry is separated by a double line space.
- If you need to cite two (or more) pieces of work published within the same year by the same author, then the convention is to refer to these texts as 2005a, 2005b and so on.
- In some interpretations of this method the first line of every entry is indented five character spaces from the left margin. However, this can create an untidy page where it is difficult to identify the author quickly.

Table 18.3(a) Outline of the Modern Languages Association (MLA) method for citing references. This is claimed to be one of the 'big three' referencing systems used in the USA. It provides author and page information in the text, but no date is included within the text, only the page number(s).

How to cite the reference in the text	How to lay out the reference list or bibliography
The cause of European integration has been further hampered by the conflict between competing interests in a range of economic activities (Roche 180). However, Hobart and Lyon have argued that this is a symptom of a wider disharmony which has its roots in socio-economic divisions arising from differing cultural attitudes towards the concept of the market economy (101). Morrison *et al.* have identified 'black market' economic activity in post-reunification Germany as one which exemplified this most markedly (99–101). Scott suggests that the black economy which existed prior to reunification operated on strong market economy principles (83). However, Main has supported the view that black market economies are not culture dependent (cited in Kay 74). Statistics presented by Johannes suggest that, in the UK, as many as 23 per cent of the population are engaged at any one time as part of the black economy (121). European-wide statistics indicate that figures for participation in the black economy may be as high as 30 per cent (Brandt 12).	Brandt, K-H. 'Working the System.' 31 December 2000. 1 April 2001. <http://www.hvn.ac.uk/econ/trickco.htm> Hobart, K. and A. Lyon, *Socio-economic Divisions: the cultural impact.* London: Thames Press, 2002. Johannes, B. 'Functional Economics.' *The Naked Economy.* M. Edouard. Cologne: Rhein Verlag, 2000: 120-30. Kay, W. *The Power of Europe.* Dover: Kentish Press, 2004. Morrison, F., *et al. Europe of the Nations.* Edinburgh: Lothian Press, 2001. Roche, P. *European Economic Integration.* London: Amazon Press, 1993. Saunders, C. ed. *The Economics of Reality.* Dublin: Shamrock Press, 1996. Scott, R. 'Informal Integration: the case of the non-monitored economy.' *Journal of European Integration Studies* 2 (2004): 81-9. 'Where the money moves.' *Ferry Times* 12 April 1999: 24.
Quotations in the text	
The movement of money within the so-called black economy is regarded by Finance Ministers in Europe as 'a success story they could emulate' (*Ferry Times* 24). Some commentators appear to give approval to non-conventional economic activity: 'black economies build businesses' (Saunders 82).	

Table 18.3(b) How to list different types of source following the Modern Languages Association (MLA) method

Type of source material	Basic format: author surname | author initial | title | place of publication | publisher | date |
Book by one author	Roche, P. *European Economic Integration*. London: Amazon Press, 1993.
Book by two authors	Hobart, K. and Lyon, A. *Socio-economic Divisions: the cultural impact*. London: Thames Press, 2002.
Book with more than three authors	Morrison, F. *et al. Europe of the Nations*. Edinburgh: Lothian Press, 2001.
Book under editorship	Saunders, C. (ed.) *The Economics of Reality*. Dublin: Shamrock Press, 1996.
Chapter in a book	Johannes, B. 'Functional Economics.' *The Naked Economy*. M. Edouard. Cologne: Rhein Press, 2000: 120–30.
Secondary referencing – where the original text is not available and the reference relates to a citation in a text that you have read. This is the secondary source and is the one that you should cite in your reference list	Kay, W. *The Power of Europe*. Dover: Kentish Press, 2004.
Journal article	Scott, R. 'Informal Integration: the case of the non-monitored economy.' *Journal of European Integration Studies* 2 (2004): 81–9.
Newspaper article	'Where the money moves.' *Ferry Times* 12 April 1999: 24.
Internet reference	Brandt, K-H. 'Working the System.' 31 December 2000. 1 April 2001. <http://www.hvn.ac.uk/econ/trickco.htm>

Notes:
- Successive lines for the same entry are indented by five character spaces.
- If two (or more) pieces of work published within the same year by the same author are cited, then refer to these texts as 1999a, 1999b and so on.

Table 18.4(a) Outline of the Vancouver method (numeric style) for citing references. This system is widely used in Medicine and the Life Sciences, for example. In the text, numbers are positioned in brackets, that is, like this (1). These numbers relate to corresponding numbered references in the reference list. This style has the advantage of not interrupting the text with citation information. However, this means that the reader cannot readily identify the source without referring to the reference list. The Vancouver style resembles in some ways the style adopted by the Institute of Electrical and Electronic Engineers (IEEE).

How to cite the reference in the text	How to lay out the reference list or bibliography
The cause of European integration has been further hampered by the conflict between competing interests in a range of economic activities (1). However, Hobart and Lyon (2) have argued that this is a symptom of a wider disharmony which has its roots in socio-economic divisions arising from differing cultural attitudes towards the concept of the market economy. Morrison *et al*. (3) have identified 'black market' economic activity in post-reunification Germany as one which exemplified this most markedly. Scott (4) suggests that the black economy which existed prior to reunification operated on strong market economy principles. However, Kay (5) has supported the view of Main that black market economies are not culture dependent. Statistics presented by Johannes (6) suggest that, in the UK, as many as 23 per cent of the population are engaged at any one time as part of the black economy. European-wide statistics indicate that figures for participation in the black economy may be as high as 30 per cent (7).	1 Roche P. European Economic Integration. London: Amazon Press; 1993. 2 Hobart K. and Lyon A. Socio-economic Divisions: the cultural impact. London: Thames Press; 2002. 3 Morrison F., Drake C., Brunswick M. and Mackenzie V. Europe of the Nations. Edinburgh: Lothian Press; 2001. 4 Scott R. Informal Integration: the case of the non-monitored economy. Journal of European Integration Studies. 2004; 2, 81-9. 5 Kay W. The Power of Europe. Dover: Kentish Press; 2004. 6 Johannes B. Functional Economics. In Edouard M. The Naked Economy. Cologne: Rhein Verlag; 2000; pp. 120-30. 7 Brandt K-H. Working the System. 2000 [cited 1 April 2001]. Available from: http://www.hvn.ac.uk/econ/trickco.htm. 8 Where the money moves. Ferry Times. 12 April 1999; 24. 9 Saunders C. editor. The Economics of Reality. Dublin, Shamrock Press; 1996.
Quotations in the text	
The movement of money within the so-called black economy is regarded by Finance Ministers in Europe as 'a success story they could emulate' (8). According to Saunders, 'black economies build businesses' (9).	

Table 18.4(b) How to list different types of source following the Vancouver method

Type of source material	Basic format: author surname | author initial | title | place of publication | publisher | date
Book by one author	Roche P. European Economic Integration. London: Amazon Press; 1993.
Book by two authors	Hobart K. and Lyon A. Socio-economic Divisions: the cultural impact. London: Thames Press; 2002.
Book with more than three authors	Morrison F., Drake C., Brunswick M. and Mackenzie V. Europe of the Nations. Edinburgh: Lothian Press; 2001.
Book under editorship	Saunders C. editor. The Economics of Reality. Dublin: Shamrock Press; 1996.
Chapter in a book	Johannes B. Functional Economics. In Edouard, M. The Naked Economy. Cologne: Rhein Verlag; 2000; pp. 120-30.
Secondary referencing – where the original text is not available and the reference relates to a citation in a text that you have read. This is the secondary source, which is the one you cite	Kay W. The Power of Europe. Dover: Kentish Press; 2004.
Journal article	Scott R. Informal Integration: the case of the non-monitored economy. Journal of European Integration Studies. 2004; 2, 81-9.
Newspaper article	Where the money moves. Ferry Times. 12 April 1999; 24.
Internet reference	Brandt K-H. Working the System. 2000 [cited 1 April 2001]. Available from: http://www.hvn.ac.uk/econ/trickco.htm.

Notes:

- In some interpretations of this style, superscript numbers[8] are used instead of the full-size number in brackets (8) shown in the example in Table 35.4(a).
- In this system, titles are not italicised.

Table 18.5(a) Outline of the Chicago method (scientific style) for citing references. This is a footnote style of referencing that enables the reader to see the full bibliographical information on the first page the reference is made. However, subsequent references of the same source do not give the same detail. If the full bibliographical information is not given in the footnote for some reason, then a full bibliography is given at the end of the work. To save space here, this method has been laid out in single-line spacing. The *Chicago Manual of Style* (2003) stipulates double-space throughout – texts, notes and bibliography.

How to cite the reference in the text

The cause of European integration has been further hampered by the conflict between competing interests in a range of economic activities.[1] However, Hobart and Lyon[2] have argued that this is a symptom of a wider disharmony which has its roots in socio-economic divisions arising from differing cultural attitudes towards the concept of the market economy. Morrison *et al.*[3] have identified 'black market' economic activity in post-reunification Germany as one which exemplified this most markedly. Scott[4] suggests, however, that the black economy which existed prior to reunification operated on strong market economy principles, while Main[5] has supported the view that black market economies are not culture dependent. Statistics presented by Johannes[6] suggest that as many as 23 per cent of the population are engaged at any one time as part of the black economy. This does not support the findings of Hobart and Lyon,[7] but it has been suggested by Scott[8] that this is probably an exaggerated statistic which it is impossible to verify. Scott[9] estimates a more modest 10 per cent of people of working age are actively involved in the black economy. Brandt[10] has conducted research into the phenomenon of the black economies of Europe but has been unable to confirm such estimates.

[1] P. Roche, *European Economic Integration* (London: Amazon Press, 1993), 180.
[2] K. Hobart, and A. Lyon, *Socio-economic Divisions: The Cultural Impact* (London: Thames Press, 2002), 101.
[3] F. Morrison, C. Drake, M. Brunswick, and V. Mackenzie, *Europe of the Nations* (Edinburgh: Lothian Press, 2001), 99.
[4] R. Scott, 'Informal Integration: the case of the non-monitored economy,' Journal of European Integration Studies, 2 (2004): 81.
[5] K. Main, *Power, Politics and People* (Plymouth: Maritime Press Co., 2003), 74, quoted in W. Kay, *The Power of Europe* (Dover: Kentish Press, 2004) 89.
[6] B. Johannes, 'Functional Economics' in *The Naked Economy*, M. Edouard, 121 (Cologne: Rhein Verlag, 2000).
[7] Hobart and Lyon *op. cit.*, 102.
[8] Scott, *op. cit.*, 83
[9] *Ibid.*
[10] K-H. Brandt, 'Working the System.' http://www.hvn.ac.uk/econ/trickco.htm (1.4.01).

▶

Table 18.5(a) continued

Quotations in the text
The movement of money within the so-called black economy is regarded by Finance Ministers in Europe as 'a success story they could emulate'.[11]
According to Saunders, 'black economies build businesses'.[12]
[11] 'Where the money moves.' *Ferry Times*, 12 April 1999, 24. [12] C. Saunders, (ed.) *The Economics of Reality* (Dublin: Shamrock Press, 1996), 82.

How to lay out the reference list or bibliography (layout differs for the footnotes)
Brandt, K-H. 'Working the System.' Available from http://www.hvn.ac.uk/econ/trickco.htm (1.4.01).
Hobart, K. and Lyon, A., *Socio-economic Divisions: The Cultural Impact*. London: Thames Press, 2002.
Johannes, B. 'Functional Economics' in *The Naked Economy*, by M. Edouard, 120–30. Cologne: Rhein Verlag, 2000.
Main, K. *Power, Politics and People*. Plymouth: Maritime Press Co., 2003, quoted in W. Kay, *The Power of Europe*. Dover: Kentish Press, 2004.
Morrison, F., *et al. Europe of the Nations*. Edinburgh: Lothian Press, 2001.
Roche, P. *European Economic Integration*. London: Amazon Press, 1993.
Saunders, C., ed. *The Economics of Reality*. Dublin: Shamrock Press, 1996.
Scott, R. 'Informal Integration: the case of the non-monitored economy.' *Journal of European Integration Studies* 2, (2004), 81–9.
'Where the money moves,' *Ferry Times*, 12 April 1999, 24.

See opposite for Table 18.5(b).

Table 18.5(b) How to list different types of source following the Chicago method. The Chicago method uses footnote-style referencing. This table gives references as these would appear in the bibliography/reference list. Note that the layout differs for the presentation of the information in the footnotes.

Type of source material	Basic format: author initial | author surname | title | place of publication | publisher | date | page number
Book by one author	Roche, P. *European Economic Integration*. London: Amazon Press, 1993.
Book by two authors	Hobart, K. and Lyon, A. *Socio-economic Divisions: The Cultural Impact*. London: Thames Press, 2002.
Book with more than three authors	Morrison, F. *et al. Europe of the Nations*. Edinburgh: Lothian Press, 2001.
Book under editorship	Saunders, C., ed. *The Economics of Reality*. Dublin: Shamrock Press, 1996.
Chapter in a book	Johannes, B. 'Functional Economics' in *The Naked Economy*, by M. Edouard, 120-30. Cologne: Rhein Verlag, 2000.
Secondary referencing - where the original text is not available and the reference relates to a citation in a text that you have read	Main, K. *Power, Politics and People*. Plymouth: Maritime Press Co., 2003, quoted in W. Kay, *The Power of Europe*. Dover: Kentish Press, 2004.
Journal article	Scott, R. 'Informal Integration: the case of the non-monitored economy,' *Journal of European Integration Studies*, 2 (2004), 81-9.
Newspaper article	'Where the money moves.' *Ferry Times*, 12 April 1999, 24.
Internet reference	Brandt, K-H. 'Working the System.' Available from http://www.hvn.ac.uk/econ/trickco.htm (1.4.01).

Notes:
- Uses superscript numbers in the text ordered consecutively. These relate to a footnote on the same page as the reference. Where references are repeated, then a new number is assigned each time it occurs in the text.
- Some abbreviations are used in this style. The most commonly used are *op. cit.* (in the work already cited) and *ibid.* (in the same place - usually in the same place as the last fully cited reference.) Thus, in the example in Table 35.5(a) [9] relates to [8] which, in turn, relates to [4].
- In the footnotes the author's first name or initial precedes the surname.
- Second or further lines in the reference or bibliography list should be indented five character spaces.

Presentation

How to follow the relevant academic conventions

The presentation of your written work may be assessed directly and it may influence the way tutors mark the content. This chapter explains how to create a polished submission that follows the established standards of academic writing.

Key topics:
→ Overall layout
→ Cover page
→ Main text
→ Citations and references
→ Quotes and formulae
→ Quoting numbers in text
→ Figures and tables

Key terms
Analogy Assignment Citation Legend Qualitative Quantitative
Quotation

Most marks for your academic assignments will be awarded for content, which depends on:

● activities that take place *before* you write, such as researching your sources, conducting experiments or analysing the literature;

● the way you express your ideas in writing.

However, presentation is the first aspect considered by a reader and some marks will always be directly or indirectly reserved for this. As a result, the final 'production' phase can influence your overall grading. By paying attention to these 'cosmetic' details, you can improve your marks relatively easily.

Presentation involves more than layout and use of visual elements; it includes accuracy, consistency and attention to detail. For this reason it is often associated with editing and proof-reading (**Ch 16**). You'll need time to get these aspects right, so when you plan the writing-up process, you should include a final phase for tackling them. For an assignment such as a lengthy in-course essay, this could mean trying to complete the content phase at least a day ahead of the submission date.

Why does good presentation matter?

- It may be an element of the assessment.
- It helps the marker understand what you have written.
- It shows you can adopt professional standards in your work.
- It demonstrates you have acquired important skills that will transfer to other subjects and, later, employment.

→ Overall layout

This will depend on the type of academic writing you have been asked to produce – an essay, report, summary or a case study. An assignment like an essay could have a relatively simple structure: a cover page, the main essay text and a list of references. A lab report might be more complex, with a title page, abstract, introduction and sections for materials and methods, results, discussion/conclusion and references. Layouts for most types of assignment also vary slightly depending on discipline. You should research this carefully before you start to write up, by consulting the course handbook or other regulations.

→ Cover page

This is important to get right because it will create a good first impression. Your department may specify a cover-page design that is required for all submissions. If this is the case, then make sure that you follow the instructions closely, as the layout may have been constructed for a particular purpose. For example, it may aid anonymous marking or provide markers with a standard format for providing feedback.

If detailed instructions for a cover page are not given, then ensure that you provide your name and/or matriculation number at the head of your work. Where anonymous marking is applied, then your matriculation number only would be required. Add your course title and/or code. The tutor's name is also helpful. Give the question number and title of the question. The model layout in Figure 19.1 suggests one way to present the essential information neatly and clearly. Keep it simple: a cover sheet with fancy graphics will not add to your mark.

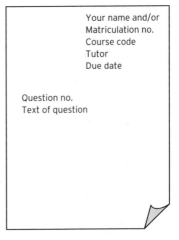

Figure 19.1 **A model cover-page layout**

→ **Main text**

The majority of student assignments are word-processed and this may be a submission requirement. You should always try to use a word processor, if you can, because this gives a more professional result and also makes the drafting and editing phases easier. However, if handwriting your submission, make sure you leave sufficient time to copy out your draft neatly and legibly. Write on only one side of the paper – this makes it easier to read, and if you make a significant error you only have to rewrite a single sheet.

Automatic wrapping of text

A point to note for computing novices is that when typing text into a word processor the words will automatically follow on to the next line (wrap). This means that you don't need to press the return key at the end of every line.

Font

There are two main choices: serif types, with extra strokes at the end of the main strokes of each letter, and sans serif types, without these strokes (see Figure 19.2). The type to use is usually left to personal

Serif font
Times roman 11 pt
Times roman 12 pt
Times roman 14 pt

Sans serif font
Arial 11 pt
Arial 12 pt
Arial 14 pt

Figure 19.2 Examples of the main types of font at different point sizes

preference. More likely to be specified is the point size (pt) of the font, which will probably be 11 or 12 point for ease of reading.

You should avoid using elaborate font types as generally they will not help the reader to assimilate what you have written. For the same reason, you should not use too many forms of emphasis. Choose *italics* or **bold** and stick with one only. Symbols are often used in academic work and in Microsoft Word can be added using the 'Insert > Symbol' menu.

Margins

A useful convention is for left-hand margins to be 4 cm and the right-hand margins 2.5 cm. This allows space for the marker's comments and ensures that the text can be read if a left-hand binding is used.

Line spacing

It is easier to read text that is spaced at least at 1.5–2 lines apart. Some markers like to add comments as they read the text and this leaves them space to do so. The exception is where you wish to use long quotations. These should be indented and typed in single-line spacing (see p. 193).

Paragraphs

The key thing to remember about layout is to make good use of the 'white space'. This means that you should lay out your paragraphs clearly and consistently. Some people prefer the indentation method, where the paragraph begins on the fourth character space from the left-hand margin (Figure 19.3a). Others prefer the blocked paragraph style, that is, where all paragraphs begin on the left-hand margin but are separated by a double-line space (Figure 19.3b). The space between paragraphs should be roughly equivalent to a missing line. In Microsoft Word these aspects can be controlled using the 'Format > Paragraph' menu.

Sub-headings

In some disciplines use of sub-headings is acceptable or even favoured, though in others these 'signpost' strategies are discouraged. It is best to consult your tutor or course handbook about this if you are uncertain. Sub-headings are usually in bold. They may also be numbered.

Punctuation

Standard punctuation applies to all types of academic writing and is dealt with in detail in **Ch 13**.

Word count

You may be asked to work to a word count and tips for doing this are provided in **Ch 16**. If you greatly exceed this limit, this will almost certainly impact on your presentation as you will confront the reader with too much information and will probably not be writing crisply and concisely.

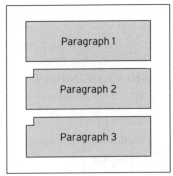

(a)

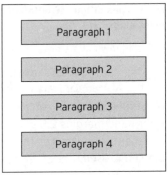

(b)

Figure 19.3 **Types of paragraph layout.** (a) indented and (b) fully justified (blocked). Note that in the indented model, by convention the first paragraph in any section is *not* indented.

→ Citations and references

A citation is mention of a source in the main body of your text – usually author surname(s) and date of publication and, in some styles, the relevant page(s). The associated reference consists of further details of the source that would, for example, allow the reader to find it in a library (see **Ch 18** for conventions). Citing authors or sources is essential within your text when you refer to ideas or quotations that are not your own. This is an important academic convention that you must observe to avoid plagiarism (**Ch 17**). Providing a reference list is, therefore, standard practice and, for this reason, markers may deduct marks if you omit one.

There are several ways in which citations can be presented, and the more common methods are outlined in **Ch 18**. References are usually listed at the end of your text in a separate section, although in some systems they may be positioned at the bottom of the page where the citation occurs. You must be consistent in the referencing style you adopt, and some disciplines impose strict subject-specific conventions. If in doubt, consult your course handbook or your lecturer.

Examples

The following is an example of a citation:

'According to Smith (2005), there are three reasons why aardvark tongues are long.'

The following is an example of a reference:

Smith, J. V., 2005. Investigation of snout and tongue length in the African aardvark *(Orycteropus afer)*. *Journal of Mammalian Research*, 34; 101–32.

→ Quotations and formulae

Quotations and formulae can be integrated into the text when short, but are usually presented as a 'special' type of paragraph when long. In both cases, the source and date of publication are provided after the quotation (p. 193).

- **Short quotations** are integrated within the sentence and are placed within single inverted commas. Quotations within the quote are in double inverted commas (Table 13.1 and Figure 19.4).

- **Long quotations** are usually 30 or more words of prose or more than two lines of poetry. They are indented by five character spaces from the left margin. No quotation marks are necessary unless there are quotation marks used in the text you are quoting (Figure 19.5).

> The cultural values identifiable in one minority group create what has been called the 'invisible clamour' (Henze, 1990) as they conflict with those of the dominant culture.

Figure 19.4 How to present a short quotation in text form

Some disciplines, for example, English Literature and Law, have very specific rules for the way in which quotations are to be laid out and referenced. In such cases, consult your course handbook or ask for guidance from a tutor.

Short formulae or equations can be included in text, but they are probably better presented on a separate line and indented, thus

$$\alpha + 4\beta / \eta^2 \, \pi = 0 \qquad \text{(Eqn. 46.1)}$$

Where a large number of formulae are included, they can be numbered for ease of cross-reference, as shown above.

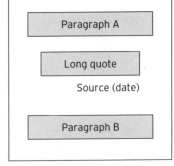

Figure 19.5 How to present a long quote, shown in outline form

→ Quoting numbers in text

Adopt the following rules:

- In general writing, spell out numbers from one to ten and use figures for 11 and above; in formal writing, spell out numbers from one to a hundred and use figures beyond this.
- Spell out high numbers that can be written in two words ('six hundred'). With a number like 4,200,000, you also have the choice of writing '4.2 million'.
- Always use figures for dates, times, currency or to give technical details ('5-amp fuse').
- Always spell out numbers that begin sentences, indefinite numbers ('hundreds of soldiers') or fractions ('seven-eighths').
- Hyphenate numbers and fractions appropriately.

→ Figures and tables

You may be expected to support your academic writing with visual material or data, and it is important that you do so in a fashion that best helps the reader to assimilate the information. You must also follow any specific presentational rules that apply in your subject area.

Figures

The academic convention is to include a wide range of visual material under the term 'Figure' ('Fig.' for short). This includes graphs, diagrams, charts, sketches, pictures and photographs, although in some disciplines and contexts photographs may be referred to as plates. Here's a set of guidelines to follow when including figures in an assignment:

- All figures should be referred to in the text. There are 'standard' formulations for doing this, such as 'Figure 4 shows that . . .'; or '. . . results for one treatment were higher than for the other (see Fig. 2)'. Find what is appropriate from the literature or texts in your subject area.

- You should always number the figures in the order they are referred to in the text. If you are including the figures within the main body of text (usually more convenient for the reader) then they should appear at the next suitable position in the text after the first time of mention. At the very least this will be after the paragraph that includes the first citation, but more normally will be at the top of the following page.

- Try to position your figures at the top or bottom of a page, rather than sandwiched between blocks of text. This looks neater and makes the text easier to read.

- Each figure should have a legend, which will include the figure number, a title and some text (often a key to the symbols and line styles used). The convention is for figure legends to appear below each figure. Your aim should be to make each figure self-contained. That is, a reader who knows the general subject area should be able to work out what your figure shows, without reference to other material.

Choosing the right *type* of figure to display information is an art in itself. Although there are technical reasons why some forms of data should be presented in particular ways (for example, proportional data in a pie chart rather than a line chart), your main focus should always be on selecting a method that will best help the reader assimilate the information presented. Jones, Reed and Weyers (2003) or the 'Chart Wizard' in the Microsoft Office Excel spreadsheet program are possible starting points for exploring the range of possibilities.

When presenting individual figures, clarity should be your main aim - ensuring, for example, that the different slices of a pie chart or the lines and symbols in a graph are clearly distinguishable from one another. Consistency is also important, so you should use the same line or shading for the same entity in all your figures (for example, hollow symbols for 'controls'). The widespread availability of colour printers should help with this, but some departments may insist on the use of black and white, since this was the convention when colour printing was prohibitively expensive. If you are using colour, keep it 'tasteful' and remember that certain colour combinations are not easily differentiated by some readers. Take great care to ensure that the quantity plotted and its units are provided for all axes.

Tables

These are used to summarise large amounts of information, in particular where a reader might be interested in some of the detail of the data. Tables are useful for qualitative textual information but numerical data can also be presented, especially if they relate to a discontinuous qualitative variable (for example, the population sizes and occupation breakdown of various geographical regions).

Tables generally include a number of columns (vertical) and rows (horizontal). By analogy with figures, the convention is to put the controlled or measured variable on the column headers (horizontal) and to place the measured variable or categories of measurement in the rows (vertical). Do not forget to include the units of the information listed if this is relevant.

The rules for presenting tables are very similar to those for figures, with the important difference that a table legend should appear above the table. It is quite common to note exceptions and other information as footnotes to tables.

Figure or table?

In certain cases it may be possible to present the same data set as a figure or as a table. The first rule in such cases is never do both – choose the method that best suits your data and the target reader. An important criterion is to decide which will best help the reader assimilate the information. If the take-home message is best shown visually, then a figure might be best; whereas, if details and numerical accuracy are important, then a table might be more suitable.

Practical tips for presenting your work

Don't let grammatical and stylistic errors spoil your work. It is a waste of effort to concentrate on presentation without also ensuring that you have ironed out minor grammatical errors at the review and proof-reading stages.

Adopt standard word-processing layout conventions. Adopting the following guidelines will ensure a neat, well-spaced presentation:

- one character space after the following punctuation – full stop, comma, colon, semicolon, closing inverted commas (double and single), question mark and exclamation mark;
- no character space after apostrophes in a 'medial' position e.g. it's, men's, monkey's;
- no indentation of paragraphs (that is, blocked style);

- one standard line space between paragraphs;
- left-justified text;
- italicised letters for foreign words and titles of books, journals and papers;
- headings in same font size as text, but bold.

Adopt figure and table styles from the literature. If you have doubts about the precise style or arrangement of figures and tables, follow the model shown in texts or journal articles from your subject area. Also, check whether relevant instructions are published in the course handbook.

Don't automatically accept the graphical output from spreadsheets and other programs. These are not always in the 'correct' style. For example, the default output for many charts produced by the Microsoft Office Excel spreadsheet includes a grey background and horizontal gridlines, neither of which is generally used. It is not difficult to alter these parts of the chart, however, and you should learn how to do this from manuals or the 'Help' facility.

(GO) And now . . .

19.1 Check for 'white' space. Look critically at your text to identify whether you have used paragraphing effectively. A useful 'trick' is to reduce the 'zoom' function on the toolbar to 25%. Your written pages will then appear in multiples on the screen which will allow you to see the overall distribution of 'white' space and length of paragraphs. This may suggest some alterations to make your text more reader-friendly.

19.2 'Personalise' your work. In many institutions the convention is for students to submit written work with only their matriculation mark as an identifier. This is done in order to facilitate anonymous marking. However, if your pages become detached for some reason, then it may be difficult for the marker to ensure that all your pages are actually included in the document that they mark. Thus, you should do three very basic things: firstly, staple all sheets together (paper clips fall off); secondly, using the View/header-footer function, insert your

▶

matriculation number in the footer, in a smaller font than the main text if you wish it to be less obtrusive; and, thirdly, insert page numbers in the footer also. This means that each page is identifiable as yours and will remain in sequence. If you are not in the habit of doing these things, then create an assignment writing template in which you insert the matriculation/identity number and page numbers. You can then use this routinely for all future written coursework.

19.3 Check out position of tables and figures. Look back at previous assignments to identify whether you have been consistent in positioning tables and figures. There is a facility within Word (Table/Properties) that allows you to position such visual elements to the left, right or centre of a page and, depending on the nature of the content, the position can make a significant difference to the reader's perception of the information.

Improving your marks

20 | Exploiting feedback

How to improve your marks by learning from what lecturers write on your work

When you receive back marked essays and assignments, they will usually be annotated by the marker. It is essential that you learn from these comments if you want to improve, but sometimes they can be difficult to understand. This chapter outlines some common annotations and describes how you should react to them.

Key topics:

→ Types of feedback
→ Examples of feedback comments and what they mean

Key terms
Formative assessment   Summative assessment

There are two principal types of assessment at university: formative and summative. Formative assessments are those in which the grade received does not contribute to your end-of-module mark, or contributes relatively little. Coursework like essays and other assignments often fall into this category. Summative assessments such as end-of-term/ -semester exams, are those which contribute directly to your final module mark. These sometimes include essays and other types of assignment such as project reports.

→ Types of feedback

The simplest pointer from any type of assessment is the grade you receive; if good, you know that you have reached the expected standard; if poor, you know that you should try to improve. If you feel unsure about the grading system or what standard is expected at each grading level, your course or faculty handbooks will probably include a description of marking or assessment criteria that explain this (see **Ch 2**).

How well are you performing?

The answer, of course, depends on your goals and expectations, but also on your understanding of degree classifications and their significance. Even in early levels of study, it may be worth relating percentage marks or other forms of grades (descriptors) to the standard degree classes – First, Upper Second, Lower Second, Third and Unclassified (**Ch 2**). Certain career and advanced degree opportunities will only be open to those with higher-level qualifications, and you should try to gain an understanding of how this operates in your field of study and likely career destination.

Written feedback may be provided directly on your essay, assignment or exam script. This will often take the form of handwritten comments over your text, and a summary commenting on your work or justifying why it received the mark it did. Sometimes the feedback will be provided separately from your work so that other markers are not influenced by it.

Some feedback may be verbal and informal, for example, a tutor's observations on an essay, or a comment about your contribution during a tutorial. If you feel uncertain about why your work has received the grade it did, or why a particular comment was provided, you may be able to arrange a one-to-one meeting with the person who marked your work. Normally they will be happy to provide further verbal explanations. However, do not attempt to haggle over your marks, other than to point out politely if it seems that part of your work does not appear to have been marked at all, or part marks appear to have been added up wrongly.

smart tip

Always read your feedback

The comments in your feedback should give you constructive direction for later efforts and are designed to help you to develop the structure and style of your work, as well as encourage you to develop a deeper understanding of the topic. Where students ignore points, especially those about presentation or structure, then they may find themselves heavily penalised in later submissions.

→ Examples of feedback comments and what they mean

Different lecturers use different terms to express similar meanings, and because they mark quickly, their handwritten comments are sometimes untidy and may be difficult to interpret. This means that you may need help in deciphering their meaning. Table 20.1 illustrates feedback comments that are frequently made and explains how you should react to obtain better grades in future. This should be viewed with Table 16.3 which explains some proof-reading symbols that lecturers may use. If a particular comment or mark does not make sense to you after reading these tables, then you may wish to approach the marker for an explanation.

Table 20.1 Common types of feedback annotation and how to act in response. Comments in the margin may be accompanied by underlining of word(s), circling of phrases, sentences or paragraphs.

Types of comment and typical examples	Meaning and potential remedial action
CONTENT	
Relevance Relevance? Importance? Value of example? So?	An example or quotation may not be apt, or you may not have explained its relevance. Think about the logic of your narrative or argument and whether there is a mismatch as implied, or whether you could add further explanation; choose a more appropriate example or quote.
Detail Give more information Example? Too much detail/ waffle/padding	You are expected to flesh out your answer with more detail or an example to illustrate your point; or, conversely, you may have provided too much information. It may be that your work lacks substance and you appear to have compensated by putting in too much description rather than analysis, for example.
Specific factual comment or comment on your approach You could have included . . . What about . . . ? Why didn't you . . . ?	Depends on context, but it should be obvious what is required to accommodate the comment.

▶

Table 20.1 continued

Types of comment and typical examples	Meaning and potential remedial action
CONTENT (continued)	
Expressions of approval *Good!* *Excellent!* ✓ (may be repeated)	You got this right or chose a good example. Keep up the good work!
Expressions of disapproval *Poor* *Weak* *No!* ✗ (may be repeated)	Sometimes obvious, but may not be clear. The implication is that your examples, logic or use of specialist language could be improved.
REGARDING STRUCTURE	
Fault in logic or argument *Logic!* *Non sequitur* (does not follow)	Your argument or line of logic is faulty. This may require quite radical changes to your approach to the topic.
Failure to introduce topic clearly *Where are you going with this?*	What is your understanding of the task? What parameters will confine your response? How do you intend to tackle the subject?
Failure to construct a logical discussion *Imbalanced discussion* *Weak on pros and cons*	When you have to compare and contrast in any way, then it is important that you give each element in your discussion equal coverage.
Failure to conclude essay clearly *So what?*	You have to leave a 'take-home message' that sums up the most salient features of your writing and you should not include new material in this section. This is to demonstrate your ability to think critically and define the key aspects.
Heavy dependency on quotations *Watch out for over-quotation* *Too many quotations*	There is a real danger of plagiarism if you include too many direct quotations from text. You have to demonstrate that you can synthesise the information from sources as evidence of your understanding. However, in a subject like English literature or law, quotation may be a key characteristic of writing. In this case, quotation is permitted, provided that it is supported by critical comment (**Ch 17** and **Ch 18**).
Move text *Loops and arrows*	Suggestion for changing order of text, usually to enhance the flow or logic.

Table 20.1 continued

Types of comment and typical examples	Meaning and potential remedial action
PRESENTATION	
Minor proofing errors *sp.* (usually in margin – spelling) *∧* (insert material here) *⌐* (break paragraph here) *⁊* (delete this material) *P* (punctuation error)	A (minor) correction is required. Table 16.3 provides more detail of likely proof-reading symbols.
Citations *Reference (required)* *Reference list omitted* *Ref!*	You have not supported evidence, argument or quotation with a reference to the original source. This is important in academic work and if you fail to do it, you may be considered guilty of plagiarism (**Ch 17**). If you omit a reference list, this will lose you marks as it implies a totally unsourced piece of writing, that is, you have done no specialist reading.
Tidiness *Illegible!* *Untidy* *Can't read*	Your handwriting may be difficult to decipher. Allocate more time to writing out your work neatly, or use a word processor if allowed.
Failure to follow recommended format *Please follow departmental template for reports* *Order!*	If the department or school provides a template for the submission of reports, then you must follow it. There are good reasons, such as the need to follow professional conventions, especially in sciences; you must conform. If you don't, then you may lose marks.

Practical tips for dealing with feedback

Be mentally prepared to learn from the views of your tutors. You may initially feel that feedback is unfair, harsh or that it misunderstands the approach you were trying to take to the question. A natural reaction might be to dismiss many of the comments. However, you should recognise that tutors probably have a much deeper understanding of the topic than you, and concede that if you want to do well in a subject then you need to gain a better understanding of what makes a good answer from the academic's point of view.

Always make sure you understand the feedback. Check with fellow students or with the lecturers involved if you cannot read the comment or do not understand why it has been made.

Respond to feedback. Make a note of common or repeated errors, even in peripheral topics, so that you can avoid them in later assignments.

(GO) And now . . .

20.1 Check out your department, school or faculty's marking criteria. As explained above, these may help you interpret feedback and understand how to reach the standard you want to achieve.

20.2 Decide what to do about feedback comments you frequently receive. For instance, do lecturers always comment about your spelling or grammar; or suggest you should use more examples; or ask for more citations to be included? If so, look at relevant chapters in this book, to see if you can adjust appropriately, or seek help from a tutor or academic support services.

20.3 Learn to criticise drafts of your own work. This is equivalent to giving feedback to yourself and is an essential academic skill. Annotate drafts of your own work – this is an important way to refine it and improve its quality. Stages you can adopt when reviewing your written work are examined in **Ch 16**.

Essay writing in exams

How to maximise your marks

The essay is a traditional method of exam assessment that allows you to discuss concepts and issues in depth. It also allows you flexibility in the way you compose your answer, and in exam situations you'll need to decide this quickly. This chapter focuses on approaches you can take to deciding on content, organising this and producing an effective answer.

Key topics:

→ What lecturers are looking for in essay answers
→ Planning essay answers in exams
→ The importance of addressing the question
→ Reviewing your answers to gain marks

Key terms

Critical thinking   Formative assessment   Instruction words
Personal pronoun   Value judgement

When you write essays and other assignments as part of your coursework assignments, you generally have a reasonable amount of time to think about and research the content, plan your approach, and construct and present your submission.

In contrast, when writing essay-style answers under exam conditions, you will not have a lengthy period to respond to the set task, and will be expected to perform under time pressure, without aids like dictionaries and thesauri and with very limited scope to review, edit and rewrite (**Ch 16**).

This chapter provides tips for writing this type of answer quickly and effectively so you can maximise the marks you obtain.

→ What lecturers are looking for in essay answers

Essay-style questions are mainly used by tutors to elicit an in-depth answer to a complex issue. Other shorter forms, such as multiple - choice or short-answer questions, tend to be included when they want you to address knowledge over a wide area, whereas the essay format allows you to develop an argument, explain alternative views or provide a high level of detail in your answer. Since you cannot be expected to know all topics in this sort of depth, there is often an element of choice in essay exam papers.

Critical thinking

Essays are commonly used when tutors expect you to think more deeply. Often what you have to do is not framed as a question but an instruction. Typically, you will be expected to:

- **apply** knowledge and understanding;
- **analyse** information;
- **synthesise** new ideas or treatments of facts;
- **evaluate** issues, positions and arguments.

See Table 7.1 for further explanation of what's expected under these headings, and watch out for instruction words that invite these approaches.

→ Planning essay answers in exams

The key tip is to keep your writing simple. Working quickly, use a concept diagram or mind map to generate ideas relevant to the question. From this, decide on an outline structure. This approach helps you to think laterally as well as in a linear manner – important so that you generate all the points relevant to your answer. As explained in **Ch 8**, you should probably think in terms of three basic components:

- **The introduction:** states briefly what your answer will say, sets its context and gives an insight as to how you intend to approach the topic.
- **The main body:** presents the information, the argument or key points of your response.

- **The conclusion:** sums up the answer as stated, reinforces the position outlined in the introduction, and puts the whole answer into a wider context.

Tips for writing these elements are provided in **Ch 8**, while potential ways of organising the main body of essay-style assignments are discussed in **Ch 9**.

Table 21.2 describes some common pitfalls that can occur when students fail to consider the structure of their writing. An important way in which marks can be lost is through poor structuring of exam answers. Ideally, your outline plan will lead to an obvious structure for the main body of the text, but often in exam situations, a piece of writing evolves once the writer begins to write. This is because the act of writing stimulates development of thought, potentially leading to changes in order and in content. In these cases, your initial outline plan should be seen as a flexible guideline that may change as you begin to think more deeply about the topic.

On the other hand, if the planning phase is ignored completely, and you only think about the structure while you write, then you can end up with a weakly structured essay. It is perfectly acceptable practice to make notes in exam books; however, you should always score through them before you submit the answer paper. A single diagonal line will suffice. Sometimes your plan may be used by the examiner to cross-check details of your answer (but do not count on this).

→ The importance of addressing the question

Another important way in which marks can be lost is when answers do not address the question (see Table 21.1). You can avoid this by:

- Making sure you consider all aspects of the question. Brainstorming techniques (**Ch 3**) can help you achieve this.
- Explaining what *you* understand by the question (perhaps in the introductory paragraph). This will make you think about the question and may clear up any doubt about how it can be interpreted. However, make sure you do not narrow the topic beyond what would be reasonable.
- Focussing on the precise task you have been asked to do (**Ch 9**). Remember to tackle the question actually asked and not the one you would have liked to answer – this is a risk of question-spotting.

- Ensuring your answer is planned. Creating a plan will make you think about relevance and the logic of your argument (**Chs 8** and **9**).

- Keeping to the point. Including irrelevant or repetitive content will not gain any marks and the time you spend writing it will be wasted, stopping you from gaining marks on other questions. Having said that, no marks are given for 'white space': even a few general points of principle may result in enough marks to help you pass, when added to those gained in other, better, answers.

Table 21.1 Checklist of possible reasons for poor exam marks in exam essays. Use this list to identify where you may have been at fault.

Reason
Not answering the exact question as set: • failing to recognise the specialist terms used in the question   • failing to carry out the precise instruction in a question   • failing to address all aspects of the question
Poor time management: • failing to match the extent of the answer(s) to the time allocated   • spending too long on one question and not enough on the others
Failing to weight parts of the answer appropriately: not recognising that one aspect (perhaps involving more complex ideas) may carry more marks than another
Failing to provide evidence to support an answer: not including examples or stating the 'obvious' – like basic facts or definitions
Failing to illustrate an answer appropriately: • not including a relevant diagram   • providing a diagram that does not aid communication
Incomplete or shallow answers: • failing to answer appropriately due to lack of knowledge   • not considering the topic in sufficient depth
Providing irrelevant evidence to support an answer: 'waffling' to fill space
Illegible handwriting: if it can't be read, it can't be marked
Poor English: facts and ideas are not expressed clearly
Lack of logic or structure to the answer: a plan not used or structure not evident
Factual errors: problems with note-taking, learning, revision or recall
Failing to correct obvious mistakes: time should be allocated for proof-reading your answer

Analysing the wording of each question

As discussed in **Ch 3**, this requires a bit more than simply thinking about *what* you are being asked to do. You need to take a broader and more in-depth look at the task in the context of the whole question. To do this, you must consider:

- **The instruction word.** In what category does that place the task? For example, have you been asked to act, describe, analyse, argue, or do something else completely (**Ch 3**)?

- **The topic.** What is the core topic about?

- **The aspect(s) to be covered.** What particular aspect of the topic has to be considered?

- **Any restriction(s).** What limits have been imposed on the discussion? Your answer must encompass each element of the task to ensure that it is a logical response to the task you were set. What you write must be relevant. Superfluous material or digressions will not earn you marks.

- Making sure you answer all parts in multi-part questions. These may not be worded in two or more sentences: phrases such as 'compare and contrast' and 'cause and effect' should alert you to this. Make sure that the weighting in marks given to questions is reflected in the length of the component parts of your answer.

- Avoiding making unsupported value judgements. These are statements that impose the writer's views on the reader, often using subjective language, and which fail to provide sound evidence to support the position put forward (**Ch 7**). Make sure you write objectively and avoid using the personal pronouns 'I', 'you', 'we' and 'one'.

Quotations and citations in exam answers

Do not become bogged down in trying to remember direct quotes word for word (possible exceptions are in literature and law exams). Just give the sense of the quote, its relevance to your answer and its source.

Table 21.2 Common faults in the structure of essay-style answers. In most of these examples, paying more attention to the planning phase will result in a better structure, and, hence, better marks.

Symptom of weakness in structure	Analysis of the problem
The magical mystery tour. This type of answer rambles on, drifting from point to disconnected point with no real structure.	The essay may contain valuable content, but marks will be lost because this is not organised and parts are not connected appropriately to create a coherent response.
No introduction and/or no conclusion. The main body contains many useful points, but fails to introduce them and fails to draw conclusions based on them.	Facts, concepts and ideas alone are not enough – evidence must be provided of deeper-level analytical thinking (**Ch 7**). The introduction and conclusions are important parts where this can be achieved.
The overly-detailed answer. The main body of the answer contains a wealth of information, some of which is relevant and some not. Despite the finely-grained detail, little structure is evident and there is no discrimination between the important and the unimportant.	The writer has probably been preoccupied with showing how much has been memorised, without showing how much has been understood. Relevance of the material in relation to the instruction given has not been considered at the planning stage, or as the essay-writing progresses.
The stream of consciousness. Often written as if it were a conversational monologue, this lacks internal organisation, few (or too many) signposting words, no (or few) paragraphs, and little apparent logic.	Academic writing style involves structural as well as linguistic components. Both are important elements of a good answer. Hence, the writing needs to guide the reader along a logical path to enable understanding.
The waffly, irrelevant answer. Unfocussed, fails to get to grips with the question and may contain large amounts of irrelevant information, offered up seemingly without regard for the topic set.	Greater attention needs to be paid to analysis of the instruction given and converting these thoughts into a coherent answer plan. Irrelevant material should not be used as it will gain no marks.
The half-an-answer. Fails to appreciate that there were two (or more) parts to the question. Focusses solely on the first part.	The essay should cover all aspects of the question as more marks may be allocated to the secondary part(s). This should be reflected in the essay plan and eventual structure.
Structure dominated by quotes. This might start with a hackneyed quote or be interspersed with extensive memorised quotes, with little effective use of these.	This type of structure leaves little room for evidence of original thought. Few marks are given for having a good memory – it's what is done with the information that counts.

→ Reviewing your answers to gain marks

This is an essential stage of creating a sound piece of academic writing, whether for an in-course assignment or exam (**Ch 20**). Many students want to get out of the exam room as soon as possible, but you should not do this unless you are convinced you have squeezed every last mark out of the paper. Your exam strategy should always include an allocation of time for reviewing. Trapping simple errors could mean the difference between a pass or a fail or between degree classifications. These are some of the things you could look for when reviewing your work (see also **Ch 16**):

- **Basics.** Make sure you have numbered your answers, answered the right number of questions, and have followed the instructions in the rubric at the start of the paper.

- **Spelling, grammar and sense.** Read through your answer critically (try to imagine it has been written by someone else) and correct any obvious errors that strike you. Does the text make sense? Do the sentences and paragraphs flow smoothly?

- **Structure and relevance.** Once again, ask yourself whether you have really answered the question that was set. Have you followed precisely the instruction(s) in the title? Is anything missed out? Are the different parts linked together well? Look for inconsistencies in argument. Add new material if necessary.

'Small-scale' corrections like spelling errors and changes to punctuation marks can be made directly in your text using standard proof-reading symbols if required (**Ch 16**).

---

smart tip

Try to to help staff to help you

It's important to realise that the person who marks your work is not an adversary. Most lecturers are disappointed when giving students a poor grade, but they approach the marking process professionally and with ruthless objectivity. Tutors are often very frustrated when they see that simple changes in approach might have led to a better mark, and they cannot assume that you know things that you do not put down on paper.

Reasons for loss of marks at advanced levels

The following are reasons why you might be marked down at higher levels of study:

- Not providing enough in-depth information.

- Providing a descriptive rather than an analytical answer – focusing on facts, rather than deeper aspects of a topic.

- Not setting a problem in context, or not demonstrating a wider understanding of the topic. However, make sure you don't overdo this, or you may risk not answering the question set.

- Not giving enough evidence of reading around the subject. This can be corrected by quoting relevant papers and reviews.

- Not considering both sides of a topic/debate, or not arriving at a conclusion if you have done so.

Practical tips for boosting your essay marks

Go in well prepared. Of course, you'd expect any lecturer to say this, because in terms of gaining good marks, there is no substitute for effective revision. However, being well prepared means more than memorising facts and concepts. To do well you also need to arrive at the exam room in a good mental state, with a plan and a positive attitude and the determination to get down to work quickly and effectively.

Have potential answer formats in mind as you go into an exam. Ideally, your revision and pre-exam preparation will have given you a good idea of the exam format and even potential exam questions. This will ensure you do not have to start answers completely from scratch.

Convert your brainstorm into a plan as quickly as possible. You can do this very quickly simply by numbering the headings in the brainstorm in the order you intend to write about them.

Keep your writing simple. If you are to stick to your exam strategy, you must not lose valuable time creating an attention-grabbing piece of writing. You won't have time or space to refine your answer in the same way as you would with a piece of coursework. In particular, don't labour the introduction with fine phrases – get straight to the point of the question and give your response to it.

Balance your effort appropriately. For example, in exam answers your introduction need not be overly long. Most marks will be awarded for the main body and conclusions, so spend more time and brainpower on them.

Focus on providing evidence of deeper thinking. Especially at higher levels of study, this will help you gain better grades. On the assumption that you are able to include basic information and display an understanding of it, you can gain marks for:

- supplying additional and relevant detail at the expected depth;
- providing an analytical answer rather than a descriptive one – focusing on deeper aspects of a topic, rather than merely recounting facts;
- setting a problem in context, and demonstrating a wider understanding of the topic; however, make sure you don't overdo this, or you may risk not answering the question set – remember that you cannot be expected to give the same amount of detail in an exam answer as you would in a piece of essay-style coursework;
- giving enough evidence of reading around the subject, by quoting relevant papers and reviews and mentioning author names and dates of publication;
- considering all sides of a topic/debate, and arriving at a clear conclusion – you may have to take into account and explain two or more viewpoints, and possibly weigh them up, according to the question set; where appropriate, your answer should demonstrate that you realise that the issue is complex and possibly unresolved.

Make sure you aren't losing marks due to poor presentation. Despite the time pressure, exam answers need to be legible and clearly laid out. If feedback indicates that tutors are having problems in reading your work, or consider it untidy, paying attention to this could be an easy way of gaining marks.

21.1 Review essay-style questions in past exam papers.
Look at these particularly from the point of view of the *depth*
of answers required. Consider both the instruction word used
(**Ch 3**) and the context to gain an appreciation of the level
of thinking demanded. Consult **Ch 7** if you need to review
'thinking processes'.

**21.2 Focus on definitions and possible formats during
revision.** If you have trouble getting your answers started
during exams, it can be a useful device to start with a definition;
alternatively, think about stating the situation, the problem and
then the potential solution. This might not be applicable to all
scenarios, but if you are really stuck this will at least give you a
framework for thinking and writing.

**21.3 Use formative assessment exercises to improve your
English.** If you recognise that your use of language is weak, then
take advantage of all formative assessment exercises to help
you improve. Speak with markers and tutors about how you
might enhance your marks. If your use of language is seen as an
impediment to your performance, seek advice from your student
advisory service. Many universities have academic writing
advisors who can help with specific writing problems.

References and further reading

BBC English Dictionary, 1992. London: BBC Worldwide Publishing.

Belbin Associates, 2006. *Belbin Team Roles* [online]. Available from: http://www.belbin.com/belbin-team-roles.htm

Bloom, B. S., Englehart, M. D., Furst, E. J., Hill, W. H. and Krathwohl, D. R., 1956. *Taxonomy of Educational Objectives: The Classification of Educational Goals. Handbook 1: Cognitive Domain*. New York: Longmans.

Chambers Dictionary, 2003. Edinburgh: Chambers Harrup Publishers Ltd.

Chicago Manual of Style, 15th edn, 2003. Chicago: University of Chicago Press.

Foley, M. and Hall, D., 2003. *Longman Advanced Learner's Grammar*. Harlow: Longman.

Fowler, H. and Winchester, S., 2002. *Fowler's Modern English Usage*. Oxford: Oxford University Press.

Jones, A. M., Reed, R. and Weyers, J. D. B., 2003. *Practical Skills in Biology*, 3rd edn. London: Pearson Education.

Longman Dictionary of Contemporary English, 2003. Harlow: Longman.

Morris, D., 2002. *Peoplewatching: The Desmond Morris Guide to Body Language*. Vintage: London.

Penguin A–Z Thesanrus, 1986. Harmondsworth: Penguin Books.

Ritter, R. M., 2005. *New Hart's Rules: The Handbook of Style for Writers and Editors*. Oxford: Oxford University Press.

Trask, R. L., 2004. *Penguin Guide to Punctuation*. London: Penguin Books.

UK Intellectual Property Office, 2007. Available from: http://www.ipo.gov.uk/copy.htm

University of Dundee, 2005. *Code of Practice on Plagiarism and Academic Dishonesty* [online]. Available from: http://www.somis.dundee.ac.uk/academic/Plagiarism.htm

Glossary of key terms

Terms are defined as used in the higher education context; many will have other meanings elsewhere. A term in **colour** denotes a cross-reference within this list.

Abbreviations:

abbr. = abbreviation

gram. = grammatical term

Latin = a word or phrase expressed in the Latin language, but not 'adopted' into English

pl. = plural

sing. = singular

vb = verb

Acronym (gram.) An abbreviation formed from the first letter of words to form a word in itself, e.g. radar, NATO.

Adjective (gram.) A word that describes a **noun**, e.g. a *tall* building.

Adverb (gram.) A word that modifies or qualifies an **adjective**, **verb** or other adverb, explaining how (manner), where (place), or when (time) an action takes place. Often adverbs end in -ly, e.g. she walked *slowly*.

Ambiguous Describes a sentence, phrase or word that could be interpreted in more than one way.

Analogy A comparison; a similar case from which parallels can be drawn.

Analyse To look at all sides of an issue, break a topic down into parts and explain how these components fit together.

Annotate To expand on given notes or text, e.g. to write extra notes on a printout of a PowerPoint presentation or a photocopied section of a book.

Anonymous marking For the purpose of assessment, the process whereby a student's paper is identified only by a matriculation/identity number, rather than by name, to avoid any potential bias in marking.

Antonym A word opposite in meaning to another.

Argue To make statements or introduce facts to establish or refute a proposition; to discuss and reason.

Assignment Coursework, usually completed in own (i.e. non-contact) time.

Bias A view or description of evidence that is not balanced, promoting one conclusion or viewpoint.

Bibliography A list of all the resources used in preparing for a piece of written work. The bibliography is usually placed at the end of a document. Compare with Reference list.

Blurb A piece of writing used as publicity, typically for a book, and appearing on the jacket or cover.

Brainstorm An intensive search for ideas, often carried out and recorded in a free-form or diagrammatic way.

Capital letter (gram.) Upper-case letter (e.g. H rather than h).

Chronological Arranged sequentially, in order of time.

Citation (1) The act of making reference to another source in one's own writing. (2) A passage or a quotation from another source provided word for word within a text. See Reference list.

Citing Quoting a reference. See Citation.

Clause (gram.) Part of sentence containing a verb. If the verb and the words relating to it can stand alone, then they comprise the *main clause*. If the words cannot stand alone, then the verb and the words that go with it form a *subordinate clause*.

Colloquial Informal words and phrases used in everyday speech (e.g. slang), and generally inappropriate for formal and academic writing.

Consonant (gram.) All letters other than the vowels.

Copyright A legally enforceable restriction of the copying and publishing of original works, allowing the author(s) or assignee(s) or their agents alone to sell copies.

Critical thinking The examination of facts, concepts and ideas in an objective manner. The ability to evaluate opinion and information systematically, clearly and with purpose.

Describe To state how something looks, happens or works.

Dewey decimal system A library catalogue system that gives each book a numerical code. Compare with Library of Congress system.

Ebrary Commercial software used to distribute and access electronic documents, such as e-books and e-journals.

Ellipsis (gram.) The replacement of words deliberately omitted from the text by three dots, e.g. 'A range of online … methods of delivering materials and resources for learning'.

Exemplify To provide an example of something.

External examiner An examiner from outside the institution whose role is to ensure that standards of examination are maintained.

Fallacy A logically erroneous argument used in reasoning or debate.

Feedback The written comments provided by the marker, usually directly on a student's coursework or exam script, or verbal comments communicated to the student.

Finger tracing The act of running your finger immediately below the line of text being read to follow your eyes' path across a page, starting and stopping a word or two from either side.

Formative assessment An assessment or exercise with the primary aim of providing feedback on performance, not just from the grade given, but also from comments provided by the examiner. Strictly, a formative assessment does not count towards a module or degree grade, although some marks are often allocated as an inducement to perform well. See Summative assessment.

Genre A particular style or category of works of art; especially a type of literary work characterised by a particular form, style or purpose.

Gist The essence of something, e.g. a summary or a list of key ideas from a piece of writing or a talk.

Glossary A list of terms and their meanings (such as this list).

Headword The main entry for a word listed in a dictionary.

Hierarchical The quality of having a set classification structure with strict guidelines of position.

Ibid. (abbr., Latin) Short for *ibidem*, meaning 'in the same place'; especially used in some referencing systems, e.g. Chicago method, when referring to the immediately previous source mentioned.

Idiom (gram.) A form of language used in everyday speech and understood by native speakers, but whose meaning is not immediately apparent from the actual words used, e.g. to 'pull someone's leg' (make them believe something that is not true).

Indentation In text layout, the positioning of text (usually three to five character spaces in) from the margin to indicate a new paragraph.

Information literacy A suite of skills that are required to find, access, analyse, create, evaluate and use information in all its formats, whether in print or online.

Instruction words The words indicating what should be done; in an exam question or instruction, the verbs or associated words that define what the examiner expects of the person answering.

Inverted commas See Quotation.

Landscape orientation The positioning of paper so that the 'long' side is horizontal. See also Portrait orientation.

Learning objective What students should be able to accomplish having participated in a course or one of its elements, such as a lecture, and having carried out any other activities, such as further reading, that are specified.

Often closely related to what students should be able to demonstrate under examination.

Learning outcome Similar to a learning objective, often focusing on some product that a student should be able to demonstrate, possibly under examination.

Legend The key to a diagram, chart or graph, e.g. showing which lines and symbols refer to which quantities.

Library of Congress system A library catalogue system that gives each book an alphanumeric code. Compare with **Dewey decimal system**.

Marking criteria A set of 'descriptors' that explain the qualities of answers falling within the differing grade bands used in assessment; used by markers to assign grades, especially where there may be more than one marker, and to allow students to see what level of answer is required to attain specific grades.

Marking scheme An indication of the marks allocated to different components of an assessment, sometimes with the rationale explained.

Mnemonic An aid to memory involving a sequence of letters or associations, e.g. 'Richard of York goes battling in vain', to remember the colours of the rainbow: red, orange, yellow, green, blue, indigo, violet.

Noun (gram.) A word denoting a person, place or thing.

Op. cit. (abbr., Latin) Short for *opus citatum*, meaning 'in the place cited'. In some forms of citation this term is used to refer to a previous citation of the same text or article.

Paraphrase To quote ideas indirectly by expressing them in other words.

Parenthesis (gram.) A word, clause, or sentence inserted as an explanation, aside, or afterthought into a passage with which it has not necessarily any grammatical connection. In writing, usually parentheses (pl.) mark off text using round brackets: (hence, more generally) an afterthought, an explanatory aside.

Perfectionism The personal quality of wanting to produce the best possible product or outcome, sometimes regardless of other factors involved.

Personal pronoun (gram.) Word referring to people. Can be first person (i.e. I), second person (i.e. she/he), or third person (i.e. they); subjective, objective and possessive. Additionally, applicable to words such as 'ship', which is referred to as 'she'.

Phonetic Relating to the sounds made in speech.

Phrasal verb (gram.) An idiomatic verbal phrase consisting of a verb and adverb or a verb and preposition. See **Idiom**.

Plagiarism Copying the work of others and passing it off as one's own, without acknowledgement.

Portrait orientation The positioning of paper so that the 'short' side is horizontal. See also Landscape orientation.

Prefix (gram.) An addition to the beginning of a word that implies a particular meaning, e.g. in the word extract, 'ex–' is a prefix meaning 'out of', which when added to 'tract' means 'to pull out of'. Compare with Suffix.

Preposition (gram.) A word that marks the relation between words or phrases, often to indicate time, place or direction, e.g. at, in, to, for. It usually comes before the word it 'controls' e.g. *at* noon; *in* the bus; *to* the north.

Primary source The source in which ideas and data are first communicated.

Prioritising Ranking tasks in precedence, taking into account their urgency and importance.

Pronoun (gram.) A word that may replace a noun: I, you, he, she, it, we, they. For example, 'Traffic lights are red, green and amber. *They* light in a particular sequence.'

Propaganda Skewed or biased reporting of the facts to favour a particular outcome or point of view.

Proper noun (gram.) The name of a place, person, organisation or singular feature, such as a river or mountain. Indicated in text with initial capital letters, e.g. 'The *Himalayas* are ...'

Qualitative Data (information) that cannot be expressed in numbers, e.g. the colour of the lecturer's tie or the quality of life of elderly patients.

Quantitative Data (information) that can be expressed in numbers, e.g. the width of the lecturer's tie or the number of elderly patients included in a survey.

Quotation Words directly lifted from a source, e.g. a journal article or book, usually placed between inverted commas (quotation marks), i.e. '...' or '...'.

Reference list A list of sources referred to in a piece of writing, usually provided at the end of the document. Compare with Bibliography.

Register (gram.) The style of language and grammar used in written or spoken form as appropriate to the context, often distinguishing formal from informal usage, for example.

Restriction The limits or bounds set on a task.

Rhetorical question A question asked as part of a talk or written work where an answer from the audience or reader is not required or expected, and indeed where the answer is usually subsequently provided by the speaker or author. Used as a device to direct the attention and thoughts of the audience or reader, e.g. 'Why is this important? I'll tell you why ...'

Secondary source A source that quotes, adapts, interprets, translates, develops or otherwise uses information drawn from primary sources.

Subject (gram.) In a sentence, the person or thing doing the action signified by the verb.

Subordinate clause (gram.) The part of a sentence that contains a verb, but would not make sense if it were to stand alone. See Clause.

Suffix (gram.) An extension at the end of a word, e.g. in the word successful, '-ful' is a suffix to the word 'success'. Compare with Prefix.

Summative assessment An exam or course assessment exercise that counts towards the final module or degree mark. Generally, no formal feedback is provided. See Formative assessment.

Superscript Text, including numerals, above the line of normal text, usually in a smaller font, e.g. ^{2}. Contrast with subscript, which is text or numerals below the line, thus $_a$.

Syllable (gram.) A unit of pronunciation larger than a single sound, but generally less than a word. In English, each syllable must contain a vowel, or a group of vowels or consonants, e.g. the syllables in 'simultaneous' are si-mul-tan-e-ous.

Syllabus The component elements of a course of study.

Synonym (gram.) A word with the same meaning as another.

Syntax (gram.) The way words are used (in their appropriate grammatical forms), especially with respect to their connection and relationships within sentences.

Tautology (gram.) A phrase that essentially and unneccesarily repeats the same thing as another, only in different words, e.g. 'the carpet was a four-sided square'.

Terminator paragraph (gram.) The paragraph that brings a piece or section of writing to an ending or conclusion.

Tense (gram.) The grammatical state of a verb that determines the timing of an event, i.e. in the past, present or the future.

Topic An area within a study; the focus of a title in a written assignment.

Topic paragraph The paragraph, usually the first, that indicates or points to the topic of a section or piece of writing and how it can be expected to develop.

Topic sentence The sentence, usually the first, that indicates or points to the topic of a paragraph and how it can be expected to develop.

Typo (abbr.) Short for typographical error – a typing mistake or, less commonly, a typesetting error.

Value judgement A statement that reflects the views and values of the speaker or writer rather than the objective reality of what is being assessed or considered.

Verbatim From Latin, meaning word for word, e.g. verbatim notes are word-for-word copies (transcriptions) of a lecture or text.

Vice versa From Latin, meaning the other way round.

Vowel (gram.) The letters a, e, i, o and u (note: y is sometimes classed as a vowel).

Writer's block The inability to structure thoughts; in particular, the inability to start the act of writing when this is required.